POTTY!

POTTY!
Clarissa's ONE POT Cookbook

CLARISSA
DICKSON WRIGHT

HODDER &
STOUGHTON

ACKNOWLEDGEMENTS

To my editor Nicky Ross for her enthusiasm; to my friend and
agent Heather Holden Brown for her tolerance and patience as
ever. And to Chloe Billington for once again dashing to the rescue.

First published as *Potty! Clarissa's One Pot Cookbook*
in Great Britain in 2010 by Hodder & Stoughton.
An Hachette UK company
This edition published in 2014

1

A CIP catalogue record for this title is available from the British Library

ISBN 978 1 444 79406 9

Photography © Howard Shooter

Illustrations by Joe McLaren

Design and Art Direction by Clare Skeats

Typeset in Skolar and Giza

Printed and bound in China by C&C Offset Printing Co. Ltd

Hodder & Stoughton policy is to use papers that are natural, renewable
and recycleable products and made from wood gown is sustainable
forests. The logging and manufacturing processes are expected to
conform to the environment regulations of the country of origin.

Hodder & Stoughton Ltd
338 Euston Road
London NW1 3BH

www.hodder.co.uk

The idea of one-pot cookery is as old as time. The minute our ancestors worked out that food tasted better cooked and started stuffing ingredients into a deer bladder to boil, it was up and running. To this day the world is full of people who for reasons of economy or limited fuel still cook their daily meals in a single pot. When China passed its per capita fuel emission tests it was due almost entirely to the wok!

Now that the recession, rising fuel costs and – to a lesser degree, if you're truthful – the future of the planet have made us concentrate on saving resources, this is perhaps the time to think of one-pot meals again. Leave behind you the era of celebrity chef, with its multiple pots and pans and huge expenditure of fuel, where everything is for show and display and not necessarily about flavour, and return to the single pot. It isn't boring and it's certainly both cheaper and easier on the washing up (more fuel saving and less use of chemicals).

For the purpose of this adventure everything cooked will be done in one dish be it wok, pressure cooker, daube or casserole. If your staple is bread, baked potato or cous cous it may be separate, and any vegetables not included will be raw (salads, crudités, and the like). If like me you live on your own or if there are just the two of you either in new romantic bliss or contented domesticity, it is much easier and in some cases quicker to use just the single pot. When I was Lord Rector of Aberdeen University my students would ask me to create delicious supper-time meals and for obvious reasons a great many of them were made as one-pot dishes.

As you will see I have tried to use my imagination to vary the type of vessels you may use for these recipes but of course you are not bound to my choice of vessel and you can use anything you have to hand – even damp newspaper! I will give a RUN Pan, my favourite choice of pan, to the reader who first sends in a dish cooked in a single vessel that I haven't used in this book.

I hope you have fun with it all.

SOUPS

Spring Vegetable Soup

This is a lovely, fresh soup for spring. It was probably historically eaten as an antiscorbutic as most people came out of the winter with incipient scurvy. It calls for the use of purslane, which has the texture of watercress and a lemony flavour. If you don't have purslane, either growing wild where you live or growing in your fields or vegetable garden, then use watercress.

Put all the ingredients except the bread and egg yolks into a large pot, cover and simmer until the vegetables are cooked. This will take about 15 minutes. Add the bread crusts to the cooking pot and simmer on a very low heat for about another 10 minutes.

Remove the soup from the heat, leave to stand for about 3–4 minutes and then stir in the egg yolks. Do this at the very last moment before serving, and do not replace on the heat. Check the seasoning and enjoy it!

Serves 4

500g (18oz) green peas, shelled (*for this recipe ideally you should use fresh green peas, but if you don't have them I find you can make it perfectly well with frozen ones*)

60g (2½oz) chervil, chopped (*if you don't have chervil, use parsley*)

100g (3½oz) purslane or watercress, chopped

1 hard lettuce, cored and shredded

250g (9oz) sorrel, shredded (*if you don't have access to sorrel, then I suggest you use lemon juice in the soup*)

3–4 onions, thinly sliced

1 tablespoon chopped parsley

1 litre (1¾ pints) water

30g (1¼oz) butter

salt and pepper

crusts of bread, as liked

2 egg yolks

Asian Soup with Dumplings

The dumplings for this soup can be made either with crab meat – tinned, frozen, ready-dressed crab, or you can of course prepare your own crab, but that is an awful lot of work just to make dumplings – or cooked prawns. It's a Nonya dish (the Nonyas are a community of Han Chinese long based in Penang and famous for their delicious cuisine) and like so many Asian soups requires a good clear stock. And for this you will have your own ready-made stock cubes to hand (see p26).

Finely shred half your bamboo shoots. Put all the ingredients for the dumplings – the pork, white fish, crab meat or prawns – into a bowl with the finely chopped garlic, the egg, soya sauce and a little salt to flavour. Add the finely shredded bamboo shoots, then oil your hands and form the mixture into dumplings, rolling them quite tightly.

Heat the oil in a saucepan and fry the remaining bamboo shoots for about 2 minutes. Pour off any excess fat, pour in the stock and bring to the boil. Gently drop in the dumplings and simmer for about 10 minutes. Season to taste and eat with gusto. You can also add glass noodles to this soup to bulk it out if you like.

Serves 4

50g (2oz) tinned bamboo shoots

300g (10½oz) minced pork

300g (10½oz) minced white fish

200g (7oz) crab meat, mixed white and brown, or finely chopped prawns

3 garlic cloves, finely chopped

1 egg

1 teaspoon light soya sauce

pinch of salt

3 tablespoons cooking oil

2 litres (3½ pints) chicken or pork stock

Indonesian Rice Soup

This is a hearty thick soup to which you can add anything within character that takes your fancy. It is eaten as a staple dish and therefore provides the whole of your meal.

Put half the rice into a heavy saucepan. Mix the meatball ingredients together with the egg yolk to bind, then form into small balls and place on top of the rice. Add half the remaining rice. Place the chicken drumsticks on top and cover with the rest of the rice. Pour on the chicken stock, season, add the chopped chilli and coriander seeds and cover tightly.

Simmer for 2 hours and serve.

Serves 4

400g (14oz) long-grain rice

4 chicken drumsticks

850ml (1½ pints) chicken stock

salt

1 chilli, chopped

1 teaspoon coriander seeds,
  roughly pounded

For the meatballs

200g (7oz) minced beef

¼ teaspoon ground cumin

¼ teaspoon ground coriander

¼ teaspoon grated nutmeg

pinch of salt

pinch of chilli flakes

1 egg yolk

Fish Soup with Almond and Fennel Seeds

This is a very agreeable soup for a warm, late spring or summer day. It's also a good way of using up whiting if you happen to have caught them, but any white fish will do.

Put the water and wine into a large saucepan and add the onion, peppercorns and fennel seeds. Cook this at a fast boil to reduce by about half. Remove from the heat, stir the almonds carefully into the mixture, then add the fish. Simmer this gently until the fish is cooked, which should take perhaps 10 minutes at the most.

When you are ready to serve, stir in the cream, the pastis and the strips of fennel and allow to heat through. Sprinkle with the chopped parsley, chives or dill.

Serves 4

500ml (18fl oz) water

500ml (18fl oz) white wine

1 large onion, thinly sliced

2 teaspoons peppercorns

2 teaspoons fennel seeds

2–3 tablespoons ground almonds

700g (1½lb) white fish, cleaned and de-boned, cut into pieces

500ml (18fl oz) double cream

3–4 teaspoons some form of pastis (*aniseed-tasting alcoholic drink like Pernod*)

½ bulb of fennel, cut into small strips

some parsley or chives or dill, chopped, for garnish

Yellow Split Pea Soup with Frankfurters

I used to make a lot of this when I went skiing in Switzerland. If I had cooked a ham for the holiday, I'd have a lot of ham stock which is particularly good in this recipe. You can use chopped ham or indeed any other sausage you like, but frankfurters or the fine wursts of Germany and Austria go best, I find. This is the most comforting of all soups.

In a large pan, fry the onion and the carrots in the oil until they are softened. Add the bay leaves. Drain the peas and add them with about two-thirds of the stock. Bring to the boil and remove any scum that comes to the surface with a slotted spoon. Add the celery leaves and simmer very gently for about 1 hour or until the peas are soft. Adjust the seasoning and add the rest of the stock. The amount depends on the consistency you like.

Cook for another 30 minutes and then add the frankfurters or whatever meat you're using, and a squeeze of lemon juice. Thin with a little water if necessary, and serve very hot.

Serves 4

1 large onion, chopped

2 carrots, sliced

3 tablespoons vegetable oil

2 bay leaves

500g (18oz) yellow split peas (*soak these overnight*)

3 litres (5¼ pints) stock (*ham if possible, otherwise chicken or beef*)

bunch of celery leaves or parsley, chopped

salt and pepper

350g (12oz) frankfurters (*whole or chopped*) or wursts or ham (*sliced*)

juice of ½ lemon

Soupe à la Déjeuner

Through much of France, soup is what is traditionally taken at lunchtime. In fact I should think that historically your average French peasant ate little other than soup. I was once reading a book called *Wild Nettle Soup* and it was then that I came to realise that in the mountains they baked all the bread for the forthcoming winter in October and then left it in the bottom drawer of a large chest where of course it hardened. This explains why, so often in French soups, you put the bread in the bottom of the bowl and pour the soup over the top of it. This strange country soup, properly known as Mourtairol, is incredibly soothing. I suppose it's the grown-up version of a bread and milk one has as children and it's basically bread melted into chicken stock.

Preheat the oven to 150°C/300°F/gas mark 2. Put the slices of bread in a casserole in layers and press them down with your hand. Dissolve the saffron into the very hot chicken stock and pour it over the bread. The bread should absorb all the liquid so that there is none swimming about.

Put the dish in the oven, cover and leave to cook for about 30 minutes. From time to time check that it is not becoming dried out and, if so, add a little more stock or even water, but do not overdo it because this should be a big, creamy mixture with practically no liquid.

I came across this soup during some time I spent in Quercy, and despite the fact that it might sound rather bland – do try it!

Serves 4

175g (6oz) rustic bread, (*either sourdough or French or Italian country bread, cut into thin slices, although it doesn't matter if you have to break it off in pieces because it will melt into the stock*)

large pinch of saffron

1 litre (1¾ pints) well-flavoured chicken stock (*and for this you really do want well-flavoured chicken stock*)

salt and pepper

Canadian Pea Soup

This is the real thing, apparently, according to my Canadian friends. There is a great addiction to this particular soup in winter and I can see why, given the frigidity of the climate in that part of the world. It's regarded as so much part of their way of life in the French quarter that its original French name is 'Soupe aux pois de l'habitant'.

Soak the peas overnight in 1.8 litres (3 pints) cold water. The next day, throw the water out and rinse the peas several times in cold running water, then put them into your soup pan with 1.2 litres (2 pints) cold water. Peel the onions and stick them with the cloves. Add these to the water together with the salt pork, the peppercorns, salt and bouquet garni. Bring the whole thing to the boil, then reduce the flame and simmer gently for 2½–3 hours. Don't put the lid on tightly, but just leave the pot half-covered.

Remove the piece of salt pork to a warm place and you can, if you want, sieve the soup or put it through a mouli. I don't usually bother, as I rather like it the way it is. If you have one of those kitchen vibrator things, that's quite a good way of dealing with it. Cut the salt pork into four pieces, put one in each soup dish and pour the soup over the top.

Serves 4

450g (1lb) whole dried peas

2 small onions

6 cloves

250g (9oz) salt pork

8 peppercorns, bruised

1 teaspoon salt

bouquet garni, made of parsley, celery tops, a bay leaf and sprig of thyme

Clam Chowder

This is a dish that exists in all its variants up and down the towns and villages of the New England coast. I believe that it came with the original settlers, the Pilgrim Fathers, from the Lincolnshire coast and was served as a communal shellfish stew. It has as many varieties as you can think of and you can add almost anything you like to it. Whatever you choose, it makes a very satisfying shared soup.

Cut the pork into 1cm (½ inch) dice and brown slowly in the pan in which you're going to cook. Fry your onions in the pork fat until they're golden brown. Wash and clean your clams (some people like to open the clams and take them out of the shells, but it's not really necessary) and throw them all in at once with the onion and pork. Add water to cover. Bring to the boil. Add all the remaining ingredients and simmer until the potatoes are just cooked.

Serve with coarse cream cracker crumbs on the side and a dash of Tabasco, if liked. One of the best ways to break the crackers into crumbs is by putting them into a plastic bag and jumping up and down on it, shouting whatever expletives against whomsoever you like. Very therapeutic!

Serves 4

250g (9oz) salt pork or bacon in one piece (*or I use coppa, which is Italian cured pork from pigs that have been fed on acorns*)

2 medium onions, chopped

4–6 dozen clams (*allowing 12–18 per person*)

2 good-sized potatoes, peeled and cut into small dice

3 large tomatoes, peeled and chopped

2 large leeks, very finely sliced

2 celery stalks, finely chopped

1 tablespoon chopped parsley

½ teaspoon thyme

2 bay leaves

generous pinch of salt

generous grinding of black pepper

slight grating of nutmeg, if you have it

Cock-a-leekie

There are a great many soups that use a whole boiling fowl. Some of them are French, but I decided that this ancient and much loved Scottish dish was the one that I would like you to think of. Traditionally this was made with an old, tough cockerel. When the alpha male in your farmyard died, it was cooked over a low peat fire overnight for the next day's supper. It's a perfect dish to cook in the very slow oven of an Aga if you have one. You can actually buy young cockerels in the late spring, and these are ideal for this. Otherwise, use a boiling fowl.

Truss your fowl and put it in a deep pan with the stock. Bring this to the boil and skim before adding the herbs and the salt and pepper. Prepare the leeks by washing and cutting each in four, lengthways, and chop into 2.5cm (1 inch) pieces, keeping the green separate from the white. Add the white of the leeks to the soup and simmer for 2–3 hours if cooking ordinarily, or as long as it takes in the slow oven of your Aga.

Add the prunes and the green of the leeks 30 minutes before serving. Lift out the fowl, remove the skin and bones and cut the meat into small pieces. Return the meat to the soup pot, correct the seasoning and eat.

Serves 4

1 fowl

3.5 litres (6 pints) beef stock

pinch of dried herbs (bay leaf, thyme, marjoram)

salt and pepper

roughly 700g (1½lb) leeks

12 prunes, soaked overnight and stoned if necessary

Fish Soup with Oranges

This is a recipe that comes from the Cadiz area of Spain and is usually made with Seville oranges or even blood oranges, which can be quite dramatic. The fish involved is hake, which the Spanish call *merluza* and are very keen on, as indeed am I. The hake has a black lining to its internal cavity, so it is best either to use fillets or to cut the fish into collops (thick pieces) where the skin is not so noticeable.

Cut the hake collops or fillets into 7.5cm (3 inch) pieces. Peel and crush the garlic clove. Heat the oil in your soup pan and add the garlic. When the garlic begins to colour, remove it and turn down the heat. Fry the onion gently until soft but not coloured.

Add the fish stock and bring back to the boil. Reduce the heat and add your hake pieces and cook them for 15–20 minutes. Then add the juice from the oranges (and lemons if you've used ordinary oranges) and check for seasoning. Serve with good rustic bread.

Serves 4

1kg (2¼lb) hake, either cut into collops or filleted

1 garlic clove

2 tablespoons olive oil

1 large onion, finely chopped

1.2 litres (2 pints) fish stock

juice of 4 Seville oranges or 3 ordinary oranges (*if you are using ordinary oranges, you also need the juice of 2 lemons*)

salt and pepper

Primordial Soup

The idea for title of this dish came about when I was at a picnic lunch at Gray's Inn – more an al fresco lunch than a picnic really – and there was a very jolly woman there called Judith Rich, who had worked for many years as a professor of biology at the Natural History Museum in London. We were discussing the origins of life and she said, 'I thought we all came from primordial soup,' and I thought, What a great title for a dish. I've played about with it in my head for ages, and got helpful remarks from my friends like, 'Use dinosaur bones – or if no dinosaur bones, use mutton,' and other such comments, but I decided that primordial was right at the beginning of time, so this is the dish I devised.

You can play about with it as much as you like; for instance, if you want to turn it into more of a meal, add noodles. If you think that primordial was murkier than this, because it's quite a clear broth, add whatever you like to make it murky. Because I was using seaweed in it, I looked at Japanese books – well, actually only one Japanese book, which was chef Shizuo Tsuji's amazing book on Japanese cooking. He's the man who has a cookery school that costs you £20,000 a year to attend.

Anyway, I'm now something of an expert on dashi, which is the clear broth that is apparently the core of all Japanese cooking. It is made by grating something that looks like a block of wood but is in fact smoked, dried bonito (a fish from the mackerel family) into your water and letting that cook. You can buy dashi in packets in Asian, Chinese and Japanese shops. However, I just used some rather good, clear fish stock and

Serves 4

1.2 litres (2 pints) good fish stock

40g (1½oz) dried kombu (*this is giant kelp*)

small piece of dried wokami seaweed (*also available in Asian shops; a substitute for this is coarsely chopped watercress*)

8 dried shrimp (*those little pink things that you get in Asian shops; alternatively use ½ teaspoon blachan, which is dried shrimp paste*)

½ teaspoon salt

1 tablespoon light soya sauce (*or slightly more if you only have the dark soya sauce*)

8 raw prawns, peeled and cut in half

noodles (optional)

the various dried seaweeds that I have in my cupboard. I also added some dried jellyfish just because it had been sitting around for a while and I wanted to use it. You don't have to do that, and indeed if you don't have any seaweed, you can always use a combination of, say, dark kale and some pak choi or one of those lighter Asian vegetables such as hollow spinach or Chinese cabbage.

Bring your fish stock to the boil and then turn down to a simmer. Do not add any of the ingredients while the stock is boiling. Once it has reduced to a simmer, put in your seaweeds and your dried shrimp, the salt and soya sauce and allow to cook for about 5 minutes. Then add your raw prawns and noodles (if using) and cook gently until the prawns are cooked through. Serve at once.

Experiment with this recipe as much as you like and remember that a primordial soup will kick off an excellent dinner party conversation. If you are using dried jellyfish, soak it and add it when you add the seaweed.

Minestrone

I am told by my Italian friends that Minestrone simply means 'soup' and that it varies from province to city to town. The one I particularly like is the Milanese version, which is made with lots of fresh, young vegetables and can be served hot or cold. It should be thick with vegetables.

Bring the stock to the boil. Add all the ingredients, except the spinach, which can be added at the very end, and simmer as gently as possible until the vegetables are tender and have absorbed nearly all the stock. Taste for seasoning and add some more beef stock to make the soup the consistency you like. Serve in heated soup plates and scatter grated Parmesan cheese on top.

Serves 4

1.2 litres (2 pints) good beef stock

50g (2oz) bacon or salt pork, cut into 2.5cm (1 inch) pieces

225g (½lb) fresh kidney or borlotti beans (*tinned or frozen are fine*)

225g (½lb) peas (*again, tinned or frozen are fine*)

1 celery stalk, scraped and diced

100g (3½oz) young cabbage, shredded

1 small onion, thinly sliced

2 medium-sized fresh tomatoes, peeled and chopped, or 200g (7oz) tin of tomatoes, without the juice

sprig of sage

50g (2oz) uncooked rice or macaroni, spaghetti or some other pasta, broken into small pieces; or you can use both rice and pasta

100g (3½oz) fresh spinach, stems removed and the leaves shredded

salt and pepper

freshly grated parmesan, to serve

Garlic Soup with Poached Eggs

Garlic soups are found all over Spain, from the delicious cold garlic soup with almonds from Córdoba to the basic rustic soup that is really just garlic and breadcrumbs with water. This is one that Alexandre Dumas mentions in the account of his journey in Spain. Don't worry about the large amount of garlic because when you've cooked it, you're not going to go round reeking of it for days.

Preheat the oven to 160°C/325°F/gas mark 3. Heat the oil in your casserole and fry the cubes of bread until they start to go crunchy and then add the garlic. Make sure that the garlic doesn't colour. Sprinkle everything with the paprika and add the stock. At this stage, if you want, you can blend the soup or pulverise it with a kitchen vibrator, or you can just leave it as it is.

Bring the liquid to the boil then lower the heat and break the eggs into the casserole one by one. Put the dish into your preheated oven until the eggs begin to sweat slightly, which will probably take about 10 minutes. You can cook the whole thing on the top of the stove and let the eggs poach there, but I find it nicer if you finish it in the oven.

Serves 4

2 tablespoons olive oil

2 slices of country bread, cut into small cubes

4 garlic cloves, very finely chopped

1 teaspoon paprika

850ml (1½ pints) light stock

Gazpacho

This is a soup that dates back to very early times and, according to the great Spanish food writer Pepita Aris, the name means something like 'bits and pieces'. It is eaten hot or cold, but the one I love best is the traditional version eaten cold in summer.

Put the bread in a dish and pour over enough cold water to cover it. Remove the bread and squeeze it out. Put the bread, onion, garlic and cayenne into a blender with the oil and salt and purée everything together. Add the cucumber, peppers, vinegar and the tomatoes and juice. Chill overnight.

Tip in the iced water just before serving to dilute to whatever consistency you like. Serve in bowls and sprinkle with the various garnishes.

Serves 6

2 slices of crustless, stale white bread

1 onion, roughly chopped

2 garlic cloves, finely chopped

pinch of cayenne pepper

2 tablespoons olive oil

generous pinch of salt

1 cucumber, seeds removed and flesh chopped

250g (9oz) mixed red and green peppers, chopped

2 tablespoons sherry vinegar or red wine vinegar

500g (18oz) ripe red tomatoes, skinned and deseeded or 400g (14oz) tin of sieved tomatoes with their juice

700ml (1¼ pints) tomato juice

425ml (15fl oz) iced water

For the garnish

freshly fried croutons

chopped red and green peppers

4 tablespoons Spanish onion or spring onion

handful of green or black olives

A Bit About Stocks

It makes a great difference when you're making your soups and stews that you have proper stock. You can of course use stock cubes – I'd recommend Knorr as the best of them. You can buy those tubs of bouillon powder, which is much the same thing really, and you can get jars of stock in upmarket super-markets like Waitrose or in delicatessens, but the easiest and best is your own home-made stock.

What I do, with the help of a pressure cooker, is to cook up a whole lot of stock and then, taking the lid off, reduce it down until it is quite concentrated and then freeze it in ice-cube trays. You can pop out the cubes into a bag later and label them. You then have ready-made stock to which you can add liquid, extra water or wine or whatever you want when you're cooking your dish. A pressure cooker is handy for this because it takes half the normal time but you can do it in an ordinary saucepan too.

If you're making chicken stock there are two types: a boiling hen, which is not that easy to find these days unless you have a Chinese supermarket nearby, or an ordinary chicken which you're dedicating to the stock. Or, second, you can make the stock from the carcass of an already cooked chicken when you've taken the meat off it.

For the boiling fowl and the whole chicken, put it into a pan with a little bit of salt and cover with water and cook it for 1 hour, possibly 2 hours if it's a boiling fowl, until you feel that all the goodness has come out of the carcass, which you can then throw away or strip the meat off and feed it to the dogs. It won't be worth the eating because there'll be no goodness left in it. This method also applies to a raw chicken carcass from which you can take the meat to use in some other dish.

If you are using the carcass of a cooked chicken, again put it in the pan and cover with water, and add an onion just to give it a bit more body, because obviously quite a lot of the goodness has already been cooked out of the chicken, and cook it for 45 minutes.

In each case, strain the stock, leave it to stand to get cold and then return it to the pan, skimming off any excess fat. Reduce it over a high heat and, once cold, pour into your ice-cube trays. I frequently pick up a veal knuckle or a pig's trotter and put this into the pan with the chicken in any of the instances above because you get a really good, rich, gelatinous stock which is excellent for both soups and stews. You can of course use the pig's trotter or the veal knuckle on their own. If you go to a butcher, they will sell you either quite cheaply.

For beef stock go to your butcher and get some beef bones. Aged bones are good because they're pretty cheap, or you can get marrow bones or any other bones the butcher has to sell you. If you want a rich, brown stock, put the bones in a medium-hot oven and roast them for about 40 minutes, then take them out and put them into a pan, add water and boil them up. A pressure cooker is particularly useful for beef bones because it saves time and energy. Again, leave your stock to cool, skim it, reduce it and freeze it in ice-cube trays.

This means that you always have delicious stock handy in the freezer for when you start cooking your one-pot meal. And I always think the secret of a really good soup is a really good stock.

Dumplings

Various sorts of dumplings served with soup can make it a bit more interesting. Most of these you can make in one batch, stick in your freezer, then take out and add to the soup as required, which I don't think contravenes the principle of the one-pot meal. Here are some of my favourites.

French Peasant Bread Dumplings

This is the dish that kept your French peasant going throughout the cold months and will reduce your central heating bill greatly. To render chicken fat put the pieces of fat in a frying pan and let them cook gently until they give up the liquid fat. You can then drain this off and keep in the fridge for up to three months. An alternative is olive oil.

Soak the bread in cold water for about 1 hour. Drain it, squeeze it very dry and mash it in a bowl with a fork. Fry the onion in the fat until golden brown and then add the mashed bread together with the parsley, lemon rind, mixed herbs, salt and pepper. Add the beaten egg and sufficient breadcrumbs to absorb any excess liquid.

When cool enough to handle, roll the mixture into tiny balls and drop them into your boiling soup about 15–20 minutes before serving.

2 slices of day-old (or older) bread

1 tablespoon finely chopped onion

1 tablespoon rendered chicken fat

2 teaspoons finely chopped parsley

rind of 1 lemon, grated

pinch of mixed herbs

salt and pepper

1 egg, beaten

fresh breadcrumbs

Egg Balls

Add the egg yolk to the sieved eggs, then add the bread-crumbs, and season. Flour your hands and roll the mixture into tiny balls. Drop them into the boiling soup and simmer for 5–10 minutes before serving.

1 egg yolk

3 hard-boiled eggs, rubbed through a sieve

1 tablespoon fresh breadcrumbs

salt and pepper

Kreplach

My all-time favourite addition to soup is Kreplach, which are stuffed pasta dumplings from Jewish cuisine. They are something similar, I suppose, to a Chinese wonton and wonderful served, as is traditional, with chicken soup.

Work your dough ingredients together, wrap in clingfilm and allow to rest for 30 minutes.

Fry the onion in the oil until soft and then add whatever meat you are using and season with salt and pepper. Cook until it changes colour. Let it cool a little and mix with the egg and parsley.

Roll out the dough very thinly on a floured surface. You fold the sheet of dough over and over into a flattened scroll and then cut into 6.5cm (2½inch) squares. Put a teaspoonful of filling into the middle of each square and fold over diagonally, bringing one point on top of the other to make a triangle. Pinch the edges together firmly and seal tightly. Once this is done leave the dumplings to stand for 15 minutes. You can either cook them separately in boiling salted water for about 15–20 minutes or drop them directly into your chicken soup.

For the dough

1 egg

pinch of salt

about 150g (5½oz) flour

For the filling (*and you can use any filling you like*)

1 small onion, finely chopped

2 tablespoons oil

175g (6oz) lean minced meat (*I like these best with pork but obviously in the Jewish tradition they're made with beef*)

salt and pepper

1 egg

1 tablespoon finely chopped parsley

Potato Dumplings

Mix the mashed potato with the semolina. Cook the onion for 5–10 minutes with the fat or butter and add to the potato mixture. Add the parsley and season with salt and pepper. Mix in the beaten egg and gradually add enough flour to make a soft but cohesive dough. Make small dumplings from the mixture and cook in the soup for 7–10 minutes.

225g (8oz) cooked mashed potato

1 tablespoon semolina

2 teaspoons finely chopped onion

25g (1oz) bacon fat or butter

2 teaspoons chopped parsley

salt and pepper

1 egg, beaten

1–2 tablespoons flour

Knaidlach

These little dumplings, also known as matzo balls, are made with matzo meal. Matzo is the type of cream cracker water biscuit that is used during Passover when no leavened bread is kept in the kitchen. The dumplings are traditionally served only at Passover, but in more recent times have come to be eaten throughout the year. They vary from country to country and indeed from household to household. At home my grandmother's cook used to make them with chicken fat, ground almonds, grated onion and chopped parsley, with one egg beaten into the chicken fat together with a little bit of warm water, salt and pepper. But Claudia Roden gives an excellent and lighter version in her *Book of Jewish Food*, as follows.

Beat the egg whites until stiff, fold in the lightly beaten egg yolks and then the matzo meal and salt and mix until all is amalgamated. Chill for about 10 minutes, then roll into little balls and drop into the soup.

2 eggs, separated

30g (1¼oz) medium matzo meal

salt

EGGS

Spinach Stew with Eggs

This is a variant on a Provençal dish. By washing the spinach in hot water and then wringing it out, you don't break any of the rules of one-pot cooking yet still blanch the spinach, as the recipe requires (although generally I don't bother).

Wash the spinach in hot water then plunge into cold water to refresh. Drain thoroughly and squeeze out any excess moisture. Chop the spinach and set aside. Heat the oil in a flameproof casserole. Add the onion and sauté it for a minute or two without letting it brown. Add the chopped spinach and stir over a low heat for 5 minutes.

When all the excess moisture has been cooked out of the spinach, add the potatoes. Season with salt and pepper and a pinch of saffron and pour on the boiling water. Add the garlic and fennel, cover the casserole and cook over a low heat for about 30 minutes, or until the potatoes are done.

Remove the lid and break the eggs on to the surface of the mixture, making sure that they are well separated, and let them poach gently. When the eggs are set, serve the casserole with the bread.

Serves 4

1kg (2¼lb) spinach

3–4 tablespoons olive oil

1 onion, chopped

5–6 waxy potatoes, peeled and thinly sliced

salt and pepper

pinch of powdered saffron

1 litre (1¾ pints) boiling water

2 garlic cloves, chopped

1 bulb of fennel, sliced

4 eggs

slices of bread, to serve

Eggs and Kippers

This is a Moroccan dish that uses harissa, a hot pepper condiment peculiar to North African cooking and that is now easily obtainable in the better supermarkets. You can make your own with dried red chilli peppers, garlic, cumin seed, salt, pepper and olive oil, pounded in a mortar or liquidised, but it's just as easy to buy it.

Heat the oil in a frying pan, add the tomatoes, harissa, paprika, garlic and caraway seeds. Put in the kippers and pour on 250ml (9fl oz) water. Simmer the mixture for 5 minutes, then add the peppers. Continue cooking over a low heat for about 20 minutes until you have a good, thick sauce.

Correct the seasoning and break the eggs one by one into the sauce. Cook until the whites have set and serve hot with crusty bread or couscous (which simply needs to be left to swell in hot water according to the directions on the packet).

Serves 4

100ml (3½fl oz) olive oil

500g (18oz) tomatoes, skinned and sieved (*or tomato passata in a carton*)

1 tablespoon harissa (*or less according to your taste because it is quite hot*)

½ teaspoon paprika

3-4 garlic cloves, thinly sliced

½ tablespoon caraway seeds, pounded

100g (3½oz) kipper fillets, broken up

250g sweet red peppers, deseeded and diced

salt

4 eggs

Chanterelles and Eggs

This slightly curious dish of eggs and mushrooms is the only recipe I've ever come across that uses catmint. It was brought to us by a cook we had who was Italian, and it makes a very nice brunch dish, especially when chanterelles or ceps are in season.

Heat the oil in a frying pan and add the garlic and catmint. When the garlic has softened a little but not coloured, add the mushrooms, season and sauté gently for 10–15 minutes. When the liquid that the mushrooms may give out has been reabsorbed, remove the catmint and break the eggs into the pan.

Allow them to set lightly without touching them, and stir the contents of the pan just once as the dish is about to be served.

Serves 6

100ml (3½fl oz) olive oil

3 garlic cloves, lightly crushed

good-sized sprig of catmint (*if you don't like the thought of this you can use any kind of mint that you have*)

500g (18oz) small chanterelles or ceps, wiped clean with a damp cloth

salt and pepper

6 eggs

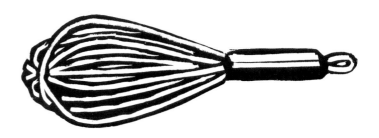

Buckwheat Pancakes with Egg and Flour

Buckwheat is the seed of a form of rhubarb that grows wild in the steppes of Asia and Russia and is much used in Central European cookery. The buckwheat pancake has more texture than an ordinary pancake and so is particularly good for this dish. It's something you'll find in the cafés and especially the truckers' cafés of northern France, and makes a very tasty single dish.

Prepare the batter by mixing the sifted flours with the salt, drop in three eggs and mix to a smooth paste with a little of the milk. Continue beating, gradually adding all the milk.

Heat a little butter or oil in a shallow frying pan and when this is hot, pour in just enough batter to cover the base in a thin layer. When the batter is cooked on the underside, loosen it with a palette knife, then crack an egg in the middle of it and scatter with a quarter of the grated cheese.

As the egg begins to cook, turn the sides of the pancake over to cover it. Then flip the whole pancake on to the other side to seal it. Make three more pancakes using the same method and serve with some form of salad.

Serves 4

250g mixed plain and buckwheat flour, sifted (*you can use up to two-thirds buckwheat flour, but you will need the ordinary flour to hold it together, I find*)

pinch of salt

7 eggs

425ml (15fl oz) milk

butter for frying or oil of some description (*it doesn't have to be olive oil*)

approx. 110g (4oz) cheese, grated

Bacon and Eggs in a Mug

When I was Lord Rector of Aberdeen University I invented this recipe for my beloved students. Working on the basis that almost anything can constitute one pot if you use it properly, this dish is literally what it says it is. It's perfect, nourishing comfort food for students or bed-sitters or just about anybody really.

Preheat the oven to 180°C/350°F/gas mark 4. Butter 4 medium-sized, heatproof mugs and sprinkle the bottom and the sides of the mugs with two-thirds of the cheese. Season the beaten eggs and divide them between the mugs. Mix the bacon, parsley and mushrooms together and spoon in a neat layer over the beaten eggs. Break an egg into each mug, season it and cover the yolk of each with 1 tablespoon cream. Cover the eggs with the remaining cheese and place a morsel of butter on top.

Put the mugs into a pan or casserole containing 4cm (1½ inches) hot water and cover loosely with foil. Cook in the oven for 10–15 minutes, until the whites of the eggs are set. The yolk should remain soft. You can also cook this dish on the hob but you will need the hot water to come up almost to the rim of the cup. Don't let the water boil, you just want a steady heat. Once the eggs are set, remove the mugs and put them under the grill for a brief moment to brown the cheese on top.

Serves 4

25g (1oz) butter

50g (2oz) grated cheese (*I use medium Cheddar for this but you can use any hard cheese you have around*)

salt and pepper

8 eggs, 4 of them broken and beaten

110g (4oz) bacon, chopped into small pieces

1 tablespoon chopped parsley

50g (2oz) mushrooms, chopped small

4 tablespoons double cream

Eggs with Cabbage

This is a versatile dish that contains everything you want for a meal, and it's very good too. You can ring the changes with the cabbage. I've come across this dish made with French beans, spring onions and even fennel, but I like it best with the cabbage.

Preheat the oven to 200°C/400°F/gas mark 6. In a pan that will go into the oven, put the cabbage, oil, onion, garlic, tomatoes and half of your fennel seeds. Cover the pan and set it over a medium heat for 20 minutes, stirring occasionally.

Remove the pan from the heat and allow it to cool slightly, then stir in half the soured cream. Make indentations in the cabbage, and break the eggs into each of these. Mix together the remaining soured cream and fennel seeds and spoon over the eggs, taking care to cover the yolks.

Cover the pan with a large sheet of buttered aluminium foil and cook in the oven for about 20 minutes, or until the whites of the eggs are set but the yolks are still runny.

Serves 4

1 savoy cabbage, outer leaves removed, then halved, cored and shredded

2 tablespoons olive oil

1 onion, thinly sliced

1 garlic clove, finely chopped

500g (18oz) ripe tomatoes, skinned and chopped

1 tablespoon fennel seeds

150ml (5fl oz) soured cream

8 eggs

Polenta with Eggs and Ham

Polenta is yellow or white coarse maize flour used as a staple in Italy and, curiously, in Eritrea where the cooking is heavily influenced by its Italian period of occupation. Buy the easy-to-prepare yellow variety and make it according to the packet instructions. White polenta is too soft for this dish.

Preheat the oven to 220°C/425°F/gas mark 7. Butter a large shallow oven dish, then cut your polenta into strips, and arrange some of these over the base. Cover this layer with bits of ham, some of the grated cheese, dabs of butter and some beaten egg.

Build it up in layers, making the strips run in different directions, lengthways and crossways, etc., until everything is used up. When you get to the last layer, cover with grated cheese and dabs of butter and cook in the oven for about 15 minutes, or until the top is golden brown.

Serves 6

450g (1lb) cooked polenta

50g (2oz) butter

275g (10oz) raw or cured ham, cut into small pieces

150g (5½oz) Parmesan cheese, grated

12 eggs, beaten

Spanish Omelette

Omelettes of any type are of course the perfect one-pot meal, the one pot in question being a large frying pan. This particular version comes from Murcia.

Heat the oil in a large frying pan and gently fry the ham, onion and green pepper for about 10 minutes. Add the aubergine and courgette and cook until all the vegetables are tender. Add the tomatoes and cook until their juice has evaporated. When the tomatoes are soft, season with a little salt and pepper.

Beat the eggs lightly with a little salt and pour them over the vegetables. Cook over a medium heat for about 2 minutes. When the underside is lightly browned, turn the omelette over and brown the other side. Alternatively, put the pan under the grill and let the top side cook. Serve in wedges with a salad of some sort.

Serves 4

100ml (3½fl oz) olive oil

100g (3½oz) ham, chopped

1 onion, diced

1 sweet green pepper, deseeded and diced

1 aubergine, peeled and diced

1 small courgette, diced

2 ripe tomatoes, skinned and chopped

salt and pepper

6–8 eggs, depending on the size of the eggs

Frittata

Here we have a rather nice recipe for a frittata, which is an Italian version of the Spanish omelette, cooked in the same way.

Heat the oil in a frying pan and when hot, cook the artichokes and aubergine, covered, over a low heat; they should take about 30 minutes to become tender. If they start to stick, add a little water. Beat the eggs in a bowl with a pinch of salt and pepper and pour over the artichokes and aubergine. Lay the strips of pepper on top of the eggs at this stage.

Cook until the eggs are set, then turn over to brown the other side. Like the Spanish omelette, you can place the frittata under a grill just to brown the top of it. Turn it out and serve cold.

Serves 4

125ml (4fl oz) olive oil

3 artichoke hearts

1 small aubergine, peeled and cut into slices, about 1cm (½ inch) thick

6 eggs

salt and pepper

2 sweet peppers, grilled, peeled and cut into thin strips (*though I tend to keep jars or tins of sweet peppers at home and use those for this omelette*)

POULTRY

Chicken with Chicory

I had a Belgian great-aunt, and the Belgians love chicory and eat a great deal of it. Aunt Emy had the best cook in Brussels – which is saying something. The measurement round her waist when she married was the measurement round her neck when she died at ninety-four. She gave me my love of chicory and this is her recipe. Don't forget to remove the core from the base of your chicory as this can be bitter.

Season the chicken and coat with flour. In a suitably sized casserole or ovenproof dish, heat the butter. Place the chicken skin side down and brown, then turn over and brown the other side. You now have the chicken skin side up.

While the chicken is browning, cut the chicory into halves and quarters, depending on size, and then put around the chicken. Cover and leave to cook gently for about 15 minutes. Then add the cream and bring to the boil. Reduce the heat again and cook for a further 30 minutes or until the chicken is cooked. Or, if you prefer, you can put the chicken into a preheated oven, 160°C/325°F/gas mark 3, to finish cooking.

Ensure the chicken is cooked through by sticking a carving fork into it and checking that the juice runs out clear. Adjust the seasoning, add the lemon juice and bring to the table.

Serves 4

1.5kg (3lb 5oz) chicken, spatchcocked (*ask your butcher to do it for you*)

salt and pepper

flour

30g (1¼oz) butter

1kg (2¼lb) chicory

500ml (18fl oz) double cream

2 teaspoons lemon juice

Isabella's Chicken

This chicken dish is Spanish in origin and used to be cooked for us at home by our cook, Isabella, who was Andalucían and married to a retired bullfighter called Carlos. It's an all-purpose dish, and very good.

Preheat the oven to 180°C/350°F/gas mark 4. Heat the olive oil in an ovenproof casserole and sauté the chicken pieces. When they are brown, add the onions and garlic and cook for a little longer, until the onion starts to soften. Add the tomatoes, artichoke hearts, red peppers, peas and a pinch of saffron. This is, of course, optional but Spanish cookery uses a lot of saffron. Season with salt and pepper, pour in the rice and stir everything together for a few minutes more.

Add the water from a boiling kettle and complete the cooking by placing the covered casserole in the oven for about 20 minutes, until the rice is virtually cooked. Remove from the oven and leave to stand for 2–3 minutes to let the rice complete its own cooking, and serve.

Serves 4

4 tablespoons olive oil

1.5 kg (3lb 5oz) chicken, cut into joints

2 onions, chopped

2 garlic cloves, finely chopped

4 tomatoes, skinned if the skins are thick, roughly chopped

4 artichoke hearts

4 sweet red peppers, deseeded and quartered

60g (2½oz) peas, frozen or freshly shelled

ground saffron (optional)

salt and pepper

300g (10½oz) long-grain rice

500ml (18fl oz) water

Chicken and Mutton

This is an old north of England dish. You can leave out the mutton if you don't have access to it, but I do recommend that you use it. I have seen versions where tomatoes are included, but I'm not going to put them in because it isn't historically correct, as tomatoes didn't come into common use until the twentieth century. The recipe really calls for a boiling fowl or a cockerel. In the late spring there are an awful lot of cockerels about as they're knocked on the head because you only need one cockerel per flock of chickens.

Put the fowl in a large casserole and arrange the mutton pieces around it. Add the onions, mushrooms, vegetable marrow, turnips and carrots. Also the garlic and salt and pepper. Pour over the cider and leave overnight. Separately soak the peas in water, also overnight.

In the morning preheat the oven to 110°C/225°F/gas mark ¼. Drain the peas and add to the casserole, then top up with water to just cover. If you're using a chicken rather than a cockerel boiling fowl, I suggest you use half stock and half water, or add a stock cube. Put the dish in the low oven and cook for the entire day.

Serves 8

1 boiling fowl or cockerel, weighing about 2kg (4lb 8oz)

750g (1lb 10oz) lean shoulder of mutton, cut into 4 pieces

4 onions, sliced

250g (9oz) mushrooms

125g (4½oz) vegetable marrow, peeled, deseeded and cubed

8 baby turnips

4 carrots, peeled and sliced

½ garlic clove, crushed

salt and pepper

400ml (14fl oz) dry cider (*if you don't have cider you can use white wine instead*)

125g (4½oz) dried split peas

In the evening, lift out the fowl and divide it into joints. You'll probably want to discard the skin. It will practically fall apart on you and not really need carving. Place the pieces of chicken on a serving dish, then carve the mutton into thick slices and put round them. Arrange the vegetables around the border.

Check the stock for seasoning and pour some of it over the dish, serving the surplus in a separate jug. If you wish, you can thicken the stock by reducing.

Duck with Sauerkraut

This is an excellent combination because the acidity of the sauerkraut takes away from the fatty richness of the duck. You can make this with wild duck as opposed to domestic duck, in which case you will need to add fat bacon, chopped into pieces.

Preheat your oven to 190°C/375°F/gas mark 5. Prick your duck all over with a carving fork and rub enthusiastically with salt and sugar. Do the salt first so that any excess is rubbed off when you are rubbing in the sugar. Work this well into any joints.

Put the duck on a trivet or rack in a shallowish casserole and cook in the oven for 30 minutes. Arrange your potatoes in the casserole around the duck, taking care to coat them in the fat, then return the dish to the oven for a further 40 minutes.

Remove the casserole from the oven and pour off any excess fat. Keep this for cooking future dishes; there's nothing nicer than duck fat. Drain the sauerkraut and arrange around the duck amid the potatoes. If the dish has a lid that fits, put it on, otherwise cover with aluminium foil and return to the oven for about another 20 minutes.

Check that the duck has cooked through and remove to a flat dish where it will be easier to carve. Serve with the sauerkraut and potatoes.

Serves 4

1 duck

salt

caster sugar

12 small potatoes or a few large potatoes cut into quarters

450g (1lb) jar of sauerkraut

Chicken with Tomatoes and Honey

This is a Moroccan dish and one you can serve with couscous, which you can steam on top of the pot with the chicken or simply pour hot water over it in a bowl and leave the grains to swell. I don't think this breaches your one-pot integrity. It's also very good with a salad.

Place the chicken or the chicken pieces in a casserole and cover with the tomatoes. Add the butter, the saffron and onion and season. Cover and cook over a moderate heat, stirring occasionally.

After about 50 minutes, when the chicken is cooked so that the flesh comes easily from the bones, remove it. Raise the heat under the casserole and continue cooking until the tomatoes have become the consistency of a thick stew and most of the liquid has evaporated. Stir frequently to prevent sticking and add the honey and cinnamon. Mix well together and cook for another 10 minutes.

Return the chicken to the casserole, turning gently so that it warms thoroughly and becomes impregnated with the rich sauce. Meanwhile, fry the almonds in a little oil. Arrange the chicken on a dish, pour over the sauce and decorate with the almonds and sesame seeds.

Serves 4

1.5kg (3lb 5oz) chicken, either left whole or cut into serving pieces

2.5kg (5lb 8oz) tomatoes, skinned, deseeded and chopped (*I tend only to skin them if the skin is very thick*)

150g (5½oz) butter, cut into pieces

generous pinch of ground saffron

1 onion, finely chopped

salt and pepper

3 tablespoons thick honey

2 teaspoons ground cinnamon

75g (3oz) blanched almonds

olive oil

1 dessertspoon toasted sesame seeds

Chicken Patty in a Gratin

This is an interesting little dish that I made up when the weather got cooler and I could actually start thinking about food again. I think it's an interesting mix of flavours that works very well and I hope you like it.

Mince your chicken or chop it very, very finely, and put it in a bowl with the breadcrumbs, the egg, parsley, chilli flakes (if using), salt and pepper, cumin powder and the finely chopped onion and garlic. Mix it all together well and form it into little patties about 5cm (2 inches) in diameter. Leave to stand for 1 hour.

Preheat the oven to 180°C/350°F/gas mark 4. In a dish that will go both on top of the hob and in the oven, heat a little olive oil and the butter and fry the chicken patties until they're just coloured. Slice the courgettes roughly, not too thin, and add these to the dish with the chicken patties. Season and pour over the tinned tomatoes. Arrange your thinly sliced potatoes over the top, dab with butter and season.

Sprinkle on the grated cheese to cover this and put into the oven for about 40 minutes, or until the top is nicely browned. Eat with salad.

Serves 4

400g (14oz) chicken fillets (*you can use both breast and thigh for this, or you could just buy a whole chicken*)

1½ slices of stale bread, crumbed

1 egg

1 tablespoon chopped flat-leaf parsley or coriander

½ teaspoon flaked chillies or cayenne pepper (optional)

salt and pepper

1 teaspoon ground cumin

1 small onion, very finely chopped

1–2 large garlic cloves, finely chopped

olive oil

25g (1oz) butter

4 courgettes

400g (14oz) tin chopped tomatoes with their juice

2 large potatoes, very thinly sliced

200g (7oz) Cheddar cheese, grated

Tangerine Chicken

I once went to Chinatown to buy my brother some wood ear mushrooms and bought what I thought was a large packet of them. Unfortunately, when I got it home and opened it up, because my Chinese is of course not fluent – in fact non-existent – it turned out to be a packet of dried tangerine skin. So we did a lot of things with tangerine skin and this is one of the recipes that came out of it. Nowadays I tend to use fresh tangerines but you can use the dried tangerine skins instead.

Joint the chicken. Zest one of the tangerines and cut the peel into thin strips. Squeeze the juice and set aside. In a wok or a heavy casserole, heat the oil and fry the garlic and the ginger gently. Raise the heat and brown the chicken pieces, carefully making sure they're all sealed. Reduce the heat and sprinkle on the Sichuan pepper, the tangerine juice, sherry and soya sauce.

Cover and cook until the chicken is just tender, probably about 25 minutes. Then add the water chestnuts, and the bamboo shoots. Add the pak choi, re-cover and cook for another 10 minutes. Add the sesame oil just before serving. If you want to use noodles add them 5–10 minutes before the end.

Serves 6

1.5kg (3lb 5oz) roasting chicken or bigger (*it can be bigger, if you wish, or you can use chicken thighs and breast fillets*)

2 tangerines or mandarins

2 tablespoons oil, not olive

2 garlic cloves, finely chopped

thumbsize piece of fresh ginger, peeled and finely chopped

1 teaspoon Sichuan pepper (*you can buy this at all good Asian delicatessens, but if you don't have it, coarsely crush some ordinary peppercorns*)

3 tablespoons orange (*if using dried peel*)

3 tablespoons dry sherry

1 tablespoon dark soya sauce

200g (7oz) tin water chestnuts, drained and cut in half

200g (7oz) tin bamboo shoots, drained and cut into pieces

3 heads of pak choi, leaves separated

1 teaspoon sesame oil

Poule au Pot

King Henry IV of France, who reigned between 1589 and 1610, must have been a remarkable man. In order to preserve his life, he had been sent away to be raised by very ordinary farming folk. When he came into his inheritance, having said that Paris was worth a Mass and thus changing his religion from Protestant to Catholic, he also declared that he wished to rule a nation where every peasant could have a chicken in the pot once a week. He was of course, as all good people are, assassinated. This is a classic Poule au Pot recipe, which is basically a stuffed chicken poached in stock with vegetables, and then served together.

For the stuffing, break the eggs into a bowl and whisk lightly. Add all the other ingredients, season and mix well together.

Loosely stuff the chicken and then truss it. Put it in a pot with the water, and bring it to the boil. If your carrots and turnips are mature, rather than old, chop them into pieces and add them at this stage. If they're young and tender, keep them on the side for a bit longer.

Cover the pot and cook over a medium heat or in a medium oven, 180°C/350°F/gas mark 4, for about 30–40 minutes, then add the young carrots and turnips and the cabbage. Continue cooking for a further 25–30 minutes, or until the chicken is done.

To serve, remove the chicken, carve it, place it on a serving dish and arrange the vegetables around it. Moisten with a few spoonfuls of stock. Serve the stock separately in a tureen, and you can add some oven-dried bread slices if you want.

Serves 4–6

2kg (4lb 8oz) chicken (*if you get it with giblets, keep the liver for the stuffing*)

2 litres (3½ pints) salted water

250g (9oz) carrots

250g (9oz) turnips

1 small cabbage with the centre stalk removed, shredded

For the stuffing

3 eggs

125g (4½oz) breadcrumbs, stale for preference

2–3 tablespoons chopped parsley

chicken liver, if you have it, chopped

60g (2½oz) each of ham and green streaky bacon, cut into dice

2–3 shallots, chopped (*if you don't have shallots use a small onion*)

salt and pepper

Kentucky Burgoo

I once gave a recipe for this to serve 500 people in my Millennium book. I have to say, I didn't test that particular recipe. Kentucky Burgoo is a very good dish and was traditionally prepared for those attending the Kentucky Derby, one of the American Triple Classics. The word 'burgoo' is a southern states' name for 'stew'.

Simmer the chicken in salted water for 1 hour or until tender. Remove the chicken, discard the bones and dice the flesh. Return to the pot with the broth and add all the other ingredients except the corn, the nutmeg and the butter. Simmer for a further 45 minutes or so, adding more water if necessary. There should be enough water to keep the vegetables covered while cooking. Stir from time to time.

Add the corn 15 minutes before the end. When the mixture begins to thicken, add the grated nutmeg and butter. Serve very hot. It's quite filling enough as it is, but it's also good served with rice, if you like, added 20 minutes before the end of the cooking time.

Serves 12

1 chicken or boiling fowl, about 2.5kg (5lb 8oz)

salt and pepper

500g (18oz) minced beef

6 bacon rashers, cut thick for preference, chopped

175g (6oz) butter beans

175g (6oz) runner beans (*or you can use French beans*), sliced

125g (4½oz) okra

6 tomatoes, chopped, skinned if the skin is thick

250g (9oz) onions, sliced

2 potatoes, diced

Tabasco sauce

1 tablespoon lemon juice

1 tablespoon sugar

175g (6oz) corn kernels scraped from the cob, or of course you can use tinned or frozen

good grating of nutmeg

30g (1¼oz) butter

Sri Lankan Curry

When I went to Sri Lanka, which was probably still called Ceylon then, it was extremely beautiful and had lovely food. This is a dish that can also be made with king prawns, but adjust the timing accordingly.

Cut the chicken into pieces. Heat the ghee or oil in a heavy casserole and fry the fenugreek seeds and curry leaves until the seeds start to pop. Add the onion, garlic and ginger and fry gently until the onion is golden. Add the turmeric, chilli, coriander and cumin and stir well. Sprinkle in the salt and vinegar, then add the sugar and stir in gently over a low heat, making sure it doesn't catch.

Add the chicken pieces to the mixture and turn so that they are evenly coated. Add the tomatoes, cardamom and cinnamon, cover and simmer over a low heat for 45 minutes. Pour in the coconut milk and cook uncovered for another 10 minutes. Remove from the heat and stir in the lime juice. Serve with nan or burritos or Asian bread.

Serves 4

1.5kg (3lb 5oz) chicken

3 tablespoons ghee or vegetable oil

¼ teaspoon fenugreek seeds

2 or 3 curry leaves

1 large onion, finely chopped

3 garlic cloves, chopped

thumbsized piece of fresh ginger, peeled and very finely chopped

1 teaspoon turmeric

2 teaspoons chilli powder

1 tablespoon ground coriander

1 teaspoon ground cumin

salt

2 tablespoons vinegar

1 teaspoon brown sugar

2 ripe tomatoes, peeled and chopped, or 200g (7oz) tin chopped tomatoes

6 cardamom pods

1 cinnamon stick

225ml (8fl oz) coconut milk

1 tablespoon lime juice

Chicken in a Clay Pot

One of the best one-pots is of course a clay pot. You want to get a good-sized clay pot so that you can put whatever vegetables you want to cook around the bird. I suppose the clay pot was an advance on cooking methods you still come across in Greece of covering a bird (usually quite a small bird) with wet clay. There's a recipe in *The Game Cookbook* for doing that with partridges and cooking them in the embers of the fire, so you can see that a clay chicken brick makes life a lot easier.

You will need to soak your pot in water for about 30 minutes before you start your cooking. You don't need to add extra water to the bird because the pot will draw out the bird's natural juices. Stuff your chicken with a nice green herb stuffing, or just leave it unstuffed if you prefer. It's a good idea to put a bed of lemon slices at the bottom of the pot before you put the bird in it.

Mix all the stuffing ingredients together in a bowl. Add a little lemon juice and stuff the mixture inside the chicken.

Lay your chicken, stuffed or unstuffed, in the clay pot on a bed of lemon slices, cover, and place it in an unheated oven, set at 230°C/450°F/gas mark 8, and allow the chicken to cook for about 1½ hours.

After the first 40 minutes open the pot and add some vegetables around the chicken; courgettes, sliced or in strips are good, as are baby new potatoes and cauliflower or broccoli florets. Cover and return the chicken to the oven and cook for the remaining time.

Serves 4

1.5kg (3lb 5oz) chicken

1 lemon, sliced

vegetables of your choice

For the stuffing

4 slices of stale bread, crust removed and roughly crumbled

1 onion, chopped

1 garlic clove

as much green herbery as you can lay your hands on: a mixture of thyme, parsley, marjoram, oregano, or anything you happen to have

handful of olives, stoned and chopped

1 dessertspoon olive oil

salt and pepper

juice of ½ lemon

Chicken in Coconut Milk

My grandmother and a lot of her family lived in Singapore and Malaya, and chicken cooked in coconut milk with peanut butter, typical of Malay cooking, was a dish we often ate. The Malays probably pounded their peanuts into a paste with a pestle and mortar, but it is much easier to use crunchy unsalted peanut butter.

Cut the chicken into pieces. Put the onions, garlic, ginger, lemongrass, chillies, coriander, turmeric, pepper, salt and curry leaves in a mortar (or you can use an electric blender). Blend all this to a paste with a little of the coconut milk. Add the peanut butter and the rest of the coconut milk and mix well. Put the chicken pieces into a large pot and pour the sauce over. Bring slowly to the boil, then turn down.

Simmer uncovered until the chicken is tender and the sauce is reduced and nicely thickened. Serve with tortillas or some sort of Asian bread.

Serves 4

1.5kg (3lb 5oz) roasting chicken

2 medium onions, chopped

2 garlic cloves, chopped

thumbsize piece of fresh ginger, peeled and chopped

2 lemongrass stalks, sliced

3 fresh red chillies (*the amount of heat is up to you; use fewer if you prefer*)

2 teaspoons ground coriander

generous pinch of ground turmeric

generous pinch of ground black pepper

salt

2–3 curry leaves

400ml (14fl oz) tin coconut milk

1 tablespoon peanut butter

Tagine of Chicken with Green Peas and Preserved Lemons

Tagines are those wonderful, pyramid-shaped, earthenware cooking pots, often in bright colours, that you find in Moroccan and Arab shops. They look attractive when brought to table, and are very good cooking vessels. You can of course use a shallow casserole dish instead.

Put your chicken pieces in a bowl and add the chopped onions, garlic, parsley, coriander, cumin and salt and pepper to taste. Add the olive oil, mix everything well and marinate for at least 2 hours or overnight.

When you are ready to cook, transfer everything to your tagine or casserole, add just enough water to cover the meat, and simmer over a low heat for 45 minutes. Add the preserved lemon peel, the peas and butter and cook for another 15 minutes.

This dish should be served with couscous, which simply needs to be put in a bowl and covered with boiling water, according to the instructions on the packet.

Serves 4

1.5kg (3lb 5oz) chicken, with the flesh cut off the bone and cut into 2.5cm (1 inch) pieces

2 large onions, chopped

2 garlic cloves, chopped

6 tablespoons chopped flat-leaf parsley

6 tablespoons chopped fresh coriander

½ teaspoon ground cumin

salt and pepper

8 tablespoons olive oil

2 preserved lemons, cut into quarters and the pulp removed

700g (1½lb) peas, fresh or frozen

3 tablespoons butter

Oven-Fried Chilli Chicken

This is a dish from *Indian Food Made Easy* by Anjum Anand, a cook whom I greatly admire and one of the few good things to be seen on television in recent years. This is a very simple dish, really designed to be eaten with your fingers, and you can serve it with any of the Asian breads you like, and a bit of yogurt, perhaps. I'm grateful to Anjum for allowing me to give the recipe and I advise you to go out and buy her books.

Blend all the marinade ingredients into a paste and place in a non-metallic bowl. Add the chicken and coat well with the paste. Leave this covered in the fridge to marinate for a couple of hours or overnight. Bring back to room temperature before cooking.

Preheat the oven to 220°C/425°F/gas mark 7. Pour the oil into a roasting tin large enough to accommodate the chicken in one layer. Heat the pan on a high shelf in the oven for 15 minutes. Mix the salt, black pepper and cumin into the breadcrumbs.

Take the chicken out of the marinade, shaking off any excess, and roll in the spicy crumbs, ensuring an even coating on all sides. Dip into the egg and add a second coating of crumbs. Place the chicken in the oiled roasting tin and cook for 20 minutes, then lower the oven temperature to 200°C/400°F/gas mark 6, turn the chicken over and cook for another 15–25 minutes, depending on the size of the pieces, or until cooked through. Serve with the lemon wedges and eat with your fingers.

Serves 6

800g (1lb 12oz) chicken joints, skinned and pierced all over with a fork

3 tablespoons vegetable oil

¼ teaspoon salt

¼ teaspoon freshly ground black pepper

¾ teaspoon ground cumin

4 slices of white bread, crumbed

1 large egg, beaten

1 lemon, cut into wedges

For the marinade

10g (½oz) fresh ginger, peeled and roughly chopped

25g (1oz) garlic, about 9 large cloves, peeled

2–4 green chillies, seeds and membranes removed

1 teaspoon salt

1 teaspoon garam masala

1 tablespoon lemon juice

2 tablespoons vegetable oil

Tablecloth Stainers (Mancha a Mantel)

This dish is named after the sauce's ability to ruin any tablecloth. It comes from the book *Two Cooks and a Suitcase* by Dougie Bell and Rhoda Robertson, who own Lupe Pinto's Deli in Edinburgh, probably the best deli for all Mexican and Central American ingredients. I've altered it slightly to make it a totally one-pot meal. The recipe calls for three different types of chillies, and you should try to get the ancho chillies, which are the sort of smoky-flavoured, not terribly hot chillies, but otherwise use whatever you can find.

Fry the onions and garlic in a little oil until soft but not coloured, then add the bacon pieces and fry until cooked. Add the chicken and fry until golden brown, turning the pieces as you go. Put in the courgettes and the plantain and fry for 5 minutes, then add the tomatoes, chicken stock, the prepared chillies and salt and pepper.

Cover and simmer for 30 minutes. Stir from time to time and mash the tomatoes into the sauce with a wooden spoon. Add the pineapple pieces 15 minutes before the end.

Check that the chicken is cooked and be sure to serve on a table without a tablecloth. Eat with flat tortillas or some other Mexican bread.

Serves 4

2 small onions, finely chopped

4 garlic cloves, crushed

oil, for frying

100g (3½oz) bacon pieces, cubed

4 chicken breast fillets, cut into cubes

2 courgettes, cubed

1 large plantain, peeled and chopped

1kg (2¼lb) fresh tomatoes, skinned, with the pips removed (*in a perfect world, these should be roasted, but don't worry*)

250ml (9fl oz) chicken stock

2 ancho chillies, soaked and the pulp removed

2 bastillas chillies, soaked and the pulp removed

2 chipotle chillies, chopped

salt and pepper

200g (7oz) fresh pineapple, cubed (*or tinned is fine*)

Paella Palenciana

I grew up with paella. One of my mother's best friends was Spanish, so we often went to Spain from when I was a small child. I had a lot of Spanish friends, and through much of my teenage years we had Spanish servants, among them our cook Isabella, who came from Valencia. Paella is arguably the best-known rice dish in the world, and really you could put almost anything in it, whatever you have to hand that's fresh; and you can vary the flavour by using pork instead of chicken, and different types of fish and shellfish. One unifying factor is that it should be cooked in either a paella pan, which is about 38.5cm (15½ inches) across, or a wide, shallow casserole. But doing it in a paella pan that is the right thickness is obviously a good idea, and it's a useful pan to have around the house.

Preheat the oven to 180°C/350°F/gas mark 4. In your paella pan, heat the olive oil over a low heat and gently cook the onions and bay leaves until the onions are soft but not coloured. Season the chicken pieces and fry them until golden. Add the broad beans and any other vegetables you're using, and stir-fry for a few minutes longer. Add a little more oil to the pan if necessary, then toss the squid rings in it until they stiffen. Season the white fish pieces and add them to the pan. Gently fry the garlic and then add the rice to the pan.

continued on page 74

Serves 6

4 tablespoons olive oil

4 medium onions, chopped

2 bay leaves

salt and pepper

1kg (2¼lb) chicken, cut into pieces

750g (1lb 10oz) broad beans (*frozen ones are fine; if the broad beans are not baby ones, take off the skin*)

anything else you happen to have in the way of French beans, celery perhaps, chopped, pea-pods or mange-tout

250g (9oz) baby squid, cleaned and cut into rings

700g (1½lb) some sort of thick, white fish, such as cod or monkfish

5 good garlic cloves, finely chopped

Stir the rice in the oil, and let it fry for 3–4 minutes, sprinkling with the paprika. Add the peas, prawns and clams or mussels and pour in a third of the hot stock. Stir again and make sure everything is evenly distributed around the pan. Cut the tomatoes into strips and arrange these on top of the rice. Add another third of the hot stock together with the white wine, reduce the heat to as low as possible and continue to cook, shifting the pan but not stirring from time to time.

Soften the saffron strands in a little warm water and stir into the dish. At this stage you can put the pan into the oven. After about 10 minutes add the remaining stock and continue cooking for another 20 minutes. Test the rice and if it's cooked, the dish is ready. Otherwise cook for a little bit longer.

You need to leave the dish to rest for about 10 minutes, covered, before you serve it, to give the rice time to absorb any extra liquid. Traditionally, it is covered with layers of newspaper, but aluminium foil will do just as well, I do assure you.

500g (18oz) risotto or Spanish paella rice

2 teaspoons paprika

75g (3oz) peas instead of or as well as your broad beans

250g (9oz) prawns, preferably in the shell

100g (3½oz) clams or mussels or some sort of mollusc of that type, cleaned

600ml (1 pint) hot stock

6 large tomatoes or 400g (14oz) tin tomatoes, drained

150ml (5fl oz) white wine

pinch of saffron powder or 20 saffron strands

Chicken in a Cauldron

This is an adaptation of a dish from Aragon, in Spain. It is very much a peasant dish. A cauldron would have hung over the fire in every cottage, gypsy encampment or shepherd's hut and would have been the main cooking vessel in all these places. Aragon was historically not a rich province until King Ferdinand married Queen Isabella of Castille and merged the two areas, so this is an old recipe. It can also be made with lamb or pork.

Rub salt and paprika into the chicken pieces. Heat the oil in a casserole and put in the chicken pieces, skin side down, and fry over a medium heat, turning until golden on all sides. Add the onion and ham and continue to fry, stirring now and again.

While they are cooking, pour boiling water over the chopped red peppers in a bowl. Soak for 10 minutes, then drain. Add them to the pan with the garlic, chopped tomatoes and chilli. Cook over a fairly high heat for 4–5 minutes.

Add the artichoke hearts and the cauliflower florets, cover the casserole and simmer until the chicken is cooked, which will be about another 20 minutes. You can also add small new potatoes, cut into quarters, to make this dish a bit more substantial.

Serves 4

salt

2 tablespoons paprika

1.5 kg (3lb 5oz) chicken, cut into pieces

2 tablespoons olive oil

1 onion, chopped

200g (7oz) smoked gammon or raw ham, diced

3 red peppers, chopped

2 garlic cloves, finely chopped

75g (3oz) tin tomatoes, drained and chopped

½ dried chilli, seeded and chopped

6 artichoke hearts, probably tinned

1 cauliflower, not too big, cut into florets

Guinea Fowl or Pheasant with Chestnuts, Red Cabbage and Baby Turnips

My friend April gives me jars of delicious pickled red cabbage which is particularly good with this dish but you won't have that benefit so, unless you have pickled red cabbage, use fresh. To save you the trouble of peeling chestnuts, or if it's the time of the year when there aren't fresh chestnuts, you can buy very good ones in vacuum packs or tins.

Preheat the oven to 180°C/350°F/gas mark 4. Heat your fat in a casserole on top of the stove and brown the pieces of your bird. Add the turnips and cook gently in the fat for a couple of minutes. Season. Shred your red cabbage, removing the core, and add to the pan with the molasses and apple. Cut the chestnuts in half and add these as well.

Pour in your ale and cook in the oven for about 1 hour. Check to see if you need to add any further liquid about halfway through the cooking. Ensure that your bird is cooked – if not leave a little longer – and serve from the casserole straight to the table.

Serves 4

oil or lard for cooking

1 guinea fowl, cut into pieces (*or 1 large or 2 small pheasants as an alternative*)

10 baby turnips, or a smaller number of slightly larger ones peeled and cut into small pieces

salt and pepper

1 small red cabbage or 225g (8oz) jar of pickled cabbage

1 dessertspoon molasses or black treacle

1 sharp-flavoured medium-sized apple, chopped

12 chestnuts

150ml (5fl oz) ale of some description (*not stout*)

Chicken and Ham Pie

One must remember, of course, that a pie as a container was the original one-pot meal. In the Middle Ages they had something like fourteen different types of pastry, many of which were not intended to be eaten but were simply a cooking pot. This pie is a double crust one, which means that the pie dish is lined at the bottom as well as being covered with pastry, and is very good eaten either hot or cold, with a salad. It is very easy to make your own pastry but if you're feeling really idle, you can buy ready-to-use pastry. This recipe uses the most basic of pastries: shortcrust. I use all butter in my shortcrust pastry but there's no doubt that using a bit of lard does give a crunchier pastry.

For the pastry, sift the flour and salt into a bowl, add the fat cut into small pieces, and rub it together with your fingers until the mixture resembles fine breadcrumbs. You can do this in a food processor but quite frankly it isn't really worth the effort. However, if you are using a food processor, operate it in short bursts until the mixture is blended, rather than keep it running. Add sufficient water to the mixture to form a firm but pliable dough. I tend to use my hands but you can use a pastry spatula if you prefer. Knead lightly, wrap in clingfilm and chill for 30 minutes.

Serves 4

1 large onion, chopped

50g (2oz) butter

40g (1½oz) flour

300ml (10fl oz) milk

½ teaspoon mustard powder

pinch of nutmeg (optional)

salt and pepper

75g (3oz) mature Cheddar cheese, grated

100g (3½oz) cooked ham, chopped

225g (8oz) cooked chicken or turkey meat

2 hard-boiled eggs, sliced

For the pastry

200g (7oz) plain flour

pinch of salt

50g (2oz) butter

50g (2oz) lard

approx. 4 tablespoons cold water

Fry the onion gently in the butter until soft. Stir in the flour and cook for 1 minute, then add the milk and bring to the boil, stirring frequently. Add the mustard and nutmeg (if using) and season. Stir in the cheese until melted, then add the ham and chicken or turkey meat and allow to cool.

Preheat the oven to 200°C/400°F/gas mark 6. Roll out two-thirds of the pastry and use it to line a shallow flan tin or pie dish about 20cm (8 inches) across. Put half the filling in your pastry case and cover with egg slices, then add the rest of the filling. Roll out the remaining pastry over the pie, position it and crimp the edges together, dampening them with water. Glaze with a little milk and bake in the oven for 35–45 minutes or until the pastry is golden. Serve hot or cold.

Pheasant and Asparagus Parcels

I have over the years eaten an enormous amount of pheasant, given to me, shot by me, all over the country. Pheasant is an excellent alternative to chicken and undoubtedly considerably healthier, unless you're very particular about where you source your chickens. Once again the pastry acts as the pot, producing a meal in itself.

Preheat the oven to 200°C/400°F/gas mark 6. Roll out your puff pastry thinly and cut into four pieces, each one large enough to enclose a pheasant breast. If you are using fresh asparagus, trim the spears well and cut each of them into two or three pieces. In a bowl, mix your mushrooms, garlic, lemon rind and juice, breadcrumbs and butter and season well.

Divide your asparagus spears between the pieces of pastry, then spoon the mushroom and breadcrumb mixture on top and add a few slices of onion. Put a pheasant breast on each pile and enclose the pheasant in the pastry, dampening the edges to seal securely. Glaze with a little milk and place on a greased baking sheet with the pastry join on the underside. Bake in the hot oven for 30–40 minutes or until the pastry is golden brown.

Serves 4

1 packet of puff pastry (*I have to confess I almost never make puff pastry; bought is perfectly good*)

350g (12oz) asparagus spears (*you can use bottled or tinned for this*)

75–100g (3–3½oz) button mushrooms, sliced

8 garlic cloves, chopped

grated rind of ½ lemon

1 tablespoon lemon juice

4 tablespoons fresh breadcrumbs

40g (1½oz) butter, cut into small pieces

salt and pepper

1 large onion, very thinly sliced

4 pheasant breasts

milk, to glaze

Pigeon with Peas

I always think this is a particularly suitable recipe for cooking pigeon because these birds can decimate your pea crop as anyone who has a garden or an allotment will know.

Place the pigeons in a pot with the peas, butter, bouquet garni and seasoning. Put on a low heat, add the flour and moisten with the stock. Cover and cook gently, either on top of the stove or in a medium oven, preheated to 160°c/325°F/gas mark 3, for about 30–40 minutes.

When the pigeons are cooked, remove them to a serving dish. Add about 1 tablespoon cooking juices to the egg yolks, then stir them into the pot together with the sugar. Let this thicken and then pour over the pigeons and serve.

Serves 4

2 pigeons, cut in half

500g (18oz) shelled young peas, or use frozen

60g (2½oz) butter

1 bouquet garni made with parsley, thyme and a bay leaf

salt and pepper

1 teaspoon flour

200ml (7fl oz) white stock

3 egg yolks

1 teaspoon sugar

FISH

Sardines and Spinach

This is a very good way of cooking fresh sardines and of course the spinach provides you with the necessary vegetables for the meal.

Preheat the oven to 220°C/425°F/gas mark 7. Remove the centre stalks from the spinach plus any other sizeable stalks and chop the leaves roughly. In a sauté pan, heat 4 tablespoons of the olive oil and lightly sauté the spinach in it. Then add the soaked bread, the garlic, parsley and salt and pepper, mix well and cook for a little bit longer.

Transfer half the spinach mixture to a bowl. Open out the sardines, skin side down, and place a spoonful of the spinach mixture on each sardine and roll up the fish round the spinach from head to tail. Half-bury the stuffed sardines in the spinach that you have left in the sauté dish with the tails upwards. Put any remaining spinach mixture around the sardines and dust with breadcrumbs. Sprinkle with the remaining oil and cook in the oven for about 10–15 minutes.

Serves 4

1kg (2¼lb) spinach

100ml (3½fl oz) olive oil

100g (3½oz) bread, soaked in milk, squeezed and crumbed

2 garlic cloves, finely chopped

2 tablespoons chopped parsley

salt and pepper

1kg (2¼lb) fresh sardines, heads removed, boned and scaled

60g (2½oz) dried breadcrumbs

Swedish Herring Gratin

This is a rather delicious dish that was the speciality of the cellar restaurant, the Opera House, in Stockholm. The dill is of course very reminiscent of all Swedish cooking and is probably the one ingredient that you can't vary. If the herrings have roes, either soft or hard, put them in as well, at the same time as the fish.

Put the sliced potatoes and onions in a shallow casserole and pour over the cream to barely cover. Crumble on your bay leaf and add your thyme and white pepper. Cook over a medium heat, covered, until the potatoes are tender (about 20 minutes).

Preheat the oven to 200°C/400°F/gas mark 6. Remove about half the potato mixture from the casserole and set aside. Sprinkle the remaining potato mix with half the dill. Arrange the herring fillets on top and sprinkle with the rest of the dill. Cover with the other half of the potato and cream mixture. Mix the breadcrumbs and cheese together and scatter this over the surface.

Dot with the butter and brown in the oven for 20 minutes or until the fish is cooked and the surface is crisp. A pickled beetroot salad goes well with this.

Serves 4

8 medium potatoes, thinly sliced

2 onions, thinly sliced

400ml (14fl oz) single cream

1 bay leaf

1 teaspoon thyme (*dried will do*)

white pepper

3 tablespoons coarsely chopped fresh dill

4 herring fillets

4 tablespoons fresh breadcrumbs

3 tablespoons grated Cheddar cheese

60g (2½oz) butter

Hake in the Spanish Manner

The Spanish are very fond of hake, which I find an excellent fish, meaty and with only the one large central bone. This is a delicious dish with crusty fresh bread, or if you wish, you could add some leftover cold new potatoes towards the end of the cooking time and let them heat through.

Preheat the oven to 180°C/350°F/gas mark 4. Heat the oil in an ovenproof dish, and fry the onions, garlic and red pepper slices. Season and stir in the paprika. Place the fish on the onions and add the tomatoes and white wine.

Cover and cook in the oven for about 40 minutes or until the fish is ready. Serve with crusty bread.

Serves 4

2 tablespoons olive oil

2 onions, thinly sliced

2 garlic cloves, chopped

1 red pepper, deseeded and thinly sliced

salt and pepper

½ teaspoon paprika

900g (2lb) piece of hake, on the bone but skin removed

6 large tomatoes, chopped, or 400g (14oz) tin chopped tomatoes

1 glass dry white wine

Gratin of Cod with Vegetables

This is based on a Norwegian dish from the port of Trondheim, right on the Arctic Circle, which is frozen in for the whole of the winter. It was given to me by a client of mine for whom I managed to get an expedited divorce, otherwise she couldn't have married her new husband because she couldn't have got into his village north of Trondheim once the ice had come. It's a dish designed for cod, but you can use haddock, ling or grey mullet for it. Or indeed any firm, white fish.

Preheat the oven to 180°C/350°F/gas mark 4. Butter a large shallow dish and line the bottom with the bread slices. Arrange the fish pieces on top and season with the salt, pepper and the other spices. Dot with a bit more butter, then spread the vegetables over the fish. Sprinkle with the parsley, cover with breadcrumbs and dot with the remaining butter.

Pour on the juice or vinegar and cook in the oven for about 40 minutes or until the fish is cooked and the topping is golden brown.

Serves 4

100g (3½oz) butter

6 slices of white bread, crusts removed

750g (1lb 10oz) cod fillets, cut into 8 equal pieces

salt and pepper

1 teaspoon paprika

1 teaspoon ground coriander

1 teaspoon ground cinnamon

¼ teaspoon ground cloves

1 medium onion, finely chopped

175g (6oz) carrots, finely chopped

175g (6oz) celeriac, roughly grated

1 tablespoon chopped parsley

2 tablespoons breadcrumbs

2 tablespoons dry grape juice, pomegranate juice or white wine vinegar

Galician Fish Pie

There was a time in my youth when my mother had a series of Spanish couples who came to work for us and who came from Galicia, which is that area of north-western Spain above Portugal, famous for its fish.

Pound the almonds in a mortar until they're a rough paste. Heat the olive oil in a sauté pan that will go in the oven and slowly cook the garlic, onions and bay leaf for about 15 minutes or until the onions are soft. Add the tomatoes, season and cook for a further 10 minutes. Add the almonds and cook for another 5-10 minutes. Remove the bay leaf.

Preheat the oven to 200°C/400°F/gas mark 6. Put the sliced potatoes in a colander, pour some boiling water over them and then refresh under a cold tap. Pour the tomato mixture into a bowl and line the bottom and sides of the sauté pan with slices of potato, leaving enough to put on the top. Then fill it with alternating layers of the tomato mixture and the fish fillets, starting with the tomato mix. Cover with the remaining potato, dot with the butter and cook in the hot oven for 40 minutes.

Serves 4

24 roughly blanched almonds

3 tablespoons olive oil

2 garlic cloves, chopped

4 medium onions, finely chopped

1 bay leaf

6 tomatoes, skinned, deseeded and chopped, or 400g (14oz) tin chopped tomatoes

salt and pepper

6 medium potatoes, peeled and very thinly sliced

500g (18oz) thin fillets of cod

30g (1¼oz) butter

Sicilian Fish Pie

This is traditionally made with swordfish, which is not always readily available in Britain, so you can use other fish, but if you can get swordfish, it's probably best. Good substitutes are anglefish, monkfish, shark, or even halibut. The great feature of this particular pie is the rather unusual pastry in which it is cooked, and which forms the pot, but if you can't be bothered to make it, then just use shortcrust.

First make the pastry. Put the flour in a bowl with the grated orange peel, a pinch of salt and the sugar and mix thoroughly. Make a well in the centre, put the egg yolks into the well and add the lard and butter. Knead until it all comes together, then form the dough into a ball, wrap it in greaseproof paper or clingfilm and leave it in the refrigerator for 1 hour.

Preheat the oven to 180°C/350°F/gas mark 4. Roll out two-thirds of your chilled pastry and use it to line a fairly deep, 23cm (9 inch) diameter mould, preferably a spring mould. Prick the bottom of the pastry all over with a fork. Mix all the ingredients (except the egg yolk) together in a bowl and put the mixture into the pie mould.

Serves 4

For the pastry

300g (10½oz) plain flour

2 tablespoons finely grated orange peel

salt

125g (4½oz) caster sugar

3 egg yolks, lightly beaten

50g (2oz) lard, cut into small pieces

125g (4½oz) butter, cut into small pieces and slightly softened

For the filling

400g (14oz) swordfish or other fish, skinned and cut into 2.5cm (1 inch) cubes

2–3 tablespoons olive oil

1 medium onion, finely chopped

1 tablespoon tomato purée

1 celery stalk, finely sliced

50g (2oz) green olives, stoned and chopped

1 tablespoon capers, rinsed and drained

Roll out the remaining dough and cover the pie with it, making sure that it is properly sealed. Make two or three cuts in the top to let the steam out. Lightly beat the egg yolk and use a pastry brush to glaze the lid.

Cook the pie in the oven for about 45 minutes or until the pastry is golden brown. Set aside to rest for a few minutes and then, sliding a knife blade round the edge, remove the pie from the cooking dish and transfer to a serving dish.

1 egg

salt and pepper

4 medium courgettes, trimmed and cut into julienne strips

10g (½oz) butter

1 egg yolk

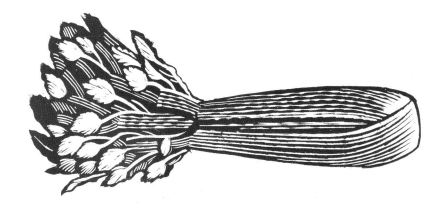

Baked Sea Bream

Sea bream are delicious fish that we slightly turn away from because they look foreign and unusual, more like a mullet in shape than a child's storybook fish. If you don't have bream, you can use snapper for this instead.

Preheat the oven to 190°C/375°F/gas mark 5. Place your fish, whole, in a greased ovenproof dish. Arrange the slices of tomato and cucumber over the fish, then mix the other ingredients together and pour over the top. Cook in the oven for about 30 minutes or until the fish is tender.

Serve with crusty bread and a well-dressed green salad.

Serves 4

1kg (2¼lb) sea bream, cleaned and scaled

3 tomatoes, sliced

½ small cucumber, sliced

1 medium onion, finely chopped

3 garlic cloves, finely chopped

1 bay leaf

2 teaspoons chopped parsley

1 sweet green pepper, cored, deseeded and finely chopped

salt and pepper

1–2 tablespoons lemon juice

2 tablespoons olive oil

Baked Sea Bass

Now that sea bass is being farmed and is so readily obtainable and relatively cheap - although not quite as tasty as the wild sea bass - this is an excellent way of cooking it. Although if you prefer you can substitute any of the bream family for the sea bass.

Put the breadcrumbs in a bowl with the milk, thyme, garlic and onion and leave to stand for about 10-15 minutes. Drain off any excess liquid and stir in the cheese. Stuff the fish with this mixture.

Preheat the oven to 180°C/350°F/gas mark 4. Make several incisions in each side of the fish. Cut the bacon rashers into thin strips and insert them into the incisions. Oil an ovenproof dish, place the fish in it and cover with the remaining bacon. Pour the stock over. The fish should be half submerged in the stock.

Cook in the oven for 50-60 minutes or until the fish is done and the flesh comes away from the bone.

Serves 4

60g (2½oz) soft breadcrumbs

100ml (3½fl oz) milk

½ teaspoon thyme

1 garlic clove, smashed into a paste

½ medium onion, finely chopped

200g (7oz) fresh, soft sheep's cheese, or use ricotta

1 large sea bass, cleaned and scaled

8 thin slices of smoked bacon

500ml (18fl oz) white stock

Gotland Fish Stew

Gotland is a Swedish island off the east coast of Sweden, and this regional dish is a good way of using flat fish. Flounder, sole of some description, or plaice are ideal, although you can use other fish instead, such as ling or cod, but in that case cut them into thin fillets.

Butter the bottom of a flameproof casserole and make alternate layers of potatoes and leeks, starting with potatoes, sprinkling each layer with chives and parsley, seasoning with salt and pepper as you go and adding a little of the horseradish. When you have finished, add enough water to cover. Cook, covered, over a low heat for 20–30 minutes or until the potatoes are almost done.

Lay the fish fillets on top and dab with butter or cover with buttered greaseproof paper. Cover the casserole and continue cooking for about another 10 minutes or until the fish is done. Adjust the seasoning and serve directly from the casserole.

Serves 4

10g (½oz) butter

5 or 6 large potatoes, sliced

2 leeks, the white part only, sliced

1 tablespoon freshly chopped chives

1 tablespoon freshly chopped parsley

salt and pepper

100g (3½oz) grated horseradish (*or if necessary you can use strong horseradish sauce*)

1kg (2¼lb) fish fillets

Grey Mullet with Walnuts

Grey mullet, though readily caught off the British coasts, tends to be scorned in our kitchens. While not having the unusual flavour of its red cousin, it is a perfectly acceptable fish to eat and just needs a little titivation. You will delight your husband if he fishes, for this is a much-caught fish. Serve this with an interesting non-lettuce salad, something like chicory or any of its relatives. You can also use sea bass for this recipe, if you can get one that's large enough.

Preheat the oven to 180°C/350°F/gas mark 4. Rub the fish well, inside and outside, with salt. Put the walnuts and garlic in a blender and pulse until they are mixed into a paste. Remove to a bowl, then add the coriander and gently pour on enough olive oil to make a rich paste. Add the lemon juice and cayenne pepper to taste.

Lay the fish on a piece of aluminium foil large enough to enclose it, and rub it well with oil. Stuff the fish with half of the walnut mixture and put the rest around the fish, inside the foil. Wrap the foil carefully around the fish and place on a baking sheet. Cook in the oven for about 40 minutes or until the fish is tender.

Serves 6

2kg (4lb 8oz) grey mullet or sea bass, or larger, cleaned

salt

125g (4½oz) walnuts

15 garlic cloves

6 sprigs of fresh coriander

250ml (9fl oz) olive oil

8 tablespoons lemon juice

cayenne pepper

Fish with Cream

This is adapted from a recipe of Jane Grigson's, which is even simpler than this version.

Preheat the oven to 400°F/200°C/gas mark 6. Butter your medium-sized gratin dish. Remove and discard the core of the fennel; thinly slice the bulbs and scatter them on top of the butter. Lay the fish on top of the fennel. Cut the potatoes into very small bits and place them around the fennel. Pour on the cream, season and give a very good, generous grinding of black pepper.

Dot the fish with a little butter and put into the hot oven until done, which will take about 20–30 minutes. If your fish fillets are particularly thin, you might put the cubes of potato into a bowl, pour boiling water over them and leave them to stand for 10 minutes before you add them to the fish.

Serves 4

10g (½oz) butter

2 bulbs of fennel

2–4 white fish fillets or steaks

2 medium potatoes

300ml (10fl oz) double cream

salt and freshly ground black pepper

Squid Stew

Where I live in Scotland, my lovely fishmonger, Mr Clark of Clark Brothers, is able to sell me better squid than you probably get in the Mediterranean. You should be able to buy squid from any fishmonger, or even a Waitrose with a good stock. This is a tasty way of cooking it. They say that there are two ways to cook squid: either you cook it very fast, or you cook it rather gently and slowly. This is one of the latter recipes.

Heat the oil in a casserole and fry the fennel slices, then add the onion, parsley, celery and fennel leaves and garlic. Cook for 2–3 minutes until the onion has begun to soften, then add the chard or spinach. Let this mixture simmer, covered, for a few minutes. Then add your squid, season and add your tomatoes.

Cover and cook gently on top of the stove until the squid is tender, which will take about 40–45 minutes.

Serves 4

3 tablespoons olive oil

1 bulb of fennel, cut into thin slices, the leaves reserved and chopped

1 onion, finely chopped

1 tablespoon finely chopped parsley

1 tablespoon chopped celery leaves

1 garlic clove, finely chopped

500g (18oz) chard or spinach leaves, ribs removed and the leaves then chopped

1.5kg (3lb 5oz) squid, cleaned, and, if they are large, cut across on the diagonal

salt and pepper

500g (18oz) tomatoes, skinned, deseeded and chopped

Vatapa

This is a famous Brazilian fish stew, which I remember eating for the first time when I was about five or six. It comes from the province of Bahia and is obviously an Afro-Brazilian dish, imported with the slaves who came to work the sugar cane.

Make up your coconut milk to 1.2 litres (2 pints) by using either water or stock, as you prefer.

In a heavy casserole, cook the onion, garlic, bay leaf and chilli peppers in 3 tablespoons olive oil for a few minutes. Add your coconut milk and water mixture and bring to the boil, then put in the fish, ground peanuts and dried shrimps. Cook this uncovered for about 20 minutes, or until the peanut and shrimp flavours have permeated the coconut milk. Add salt to taste.

Gradually stir in your cornmeal and cook this over a low heat for 30 minutes, stirring frequently to prevent scorching, until it becomes a smooth, thick mush about the consistency of double cream. At this point add the fresh prawns and the remaining oil and cook gently until the fish is cooked.

Serves 4

2 × 400g (14oz) tins coconut milk

1 onion, sliced

1 garlic clove, sliced

1 bay leaf

1–4 fresh chillies, halved, deseeded and chopped (*depending on how hot you like your food*)

5 tablespoons olive oil

500g (18oz) firm-fleshed fish, skinned and sliced

125g (4½oz) roasted peanuts, finely ground or pounded in a mortar

250g (9oz) dried shrimps or blachan (*dried shrimp paste, which you can buy in any Asian shop or Chinese delicatessen*)

salt

150g (5½oz) yellow cornmeal

500g (18oz) fresh prawns, peeled

Provençal Fish Stew

The south of France is noted for its hearty fish stews, and this is a general one to which you can add whatever fish you have, such as snappers, grey sole, lemon sole, mullet, whiting, sea bass, cod and halibut. This particular recipe calls for conger eel and soft-shell crabs, but if you can't get those or you don't want to use them just leave them out.

Spread out the fish and seafood on a large platter and sprinkle them with 4–5 tablespoons olive oil, the herbs and about half the pastis. (At this stage you can add a pinch of powdered saffron, if you happen to have it, which will give a nice colour.) Rub these well all over the fish and leave them to marinate for 1 hour.

Heat the remaining oil in a large saucepan, put in the leeks and onions and cook gently in the oil for about 10 minutes, stirring occasionally with a wooden spoon. Then add the tomatoes and the dried orange peel and cook for 5 minutes longer. Salt lightly and add a good amount of freshly ground pepper. Raise the heat under the pan and add the fish stock and the remaining pastis. From this point, it'll take you 15 minutes to finish the dish.

continued on p106

Serves 4

2kg (4lb 8oz) mixed whole fish of medium size, cleaned and scaled (red snappers, grey sole, mullet, whiting, or similar)

500g (18oz) further fish (cod, halibut, sea bass), trimmed and thickly sliced

500g (18oz) conger eel cut into 4cm (1½ inch) slices

500g (18oz) soft-shell crabs (optional)

10 prawns, peeled and the heads removed

250ml (9fl oz) olive oil

1 teaspoon mixed herbs: thyme, savory, oregano, marjoram, or whatever you choose

100ml (3½fl oz) pastis: Ricard, Pernod or Marie Brizard

500g (18oz) white parts of leeks, finely chopped

2 medium onions, finely chopped

Keep the pan over a good heat. Add the fish in three different batches: the conger eel and firm-fleshed fish should go in first, then any crustaceans. After 5 minutes add the larger specimens of the more tender-fleshed fish, such as the sole, then the smaller, soft-fleshed fish (this all depends what kind of fish you're using, so use your brains and your imagination).

While the fish is cooking, rub the dried bread slices with the cloves of garlic. Allow one medium sized clove for three slices of bread. Bring to the table and put the dried bread in the bottom of each serving bowl, and then pour over the broth and divide up the fish.

750g (1lb 10oz) well-ripened tomatoes, skinned, deseeded and chopped

1 strip of dried orange peel

salt and black pepper

2.75 litres (4¾ pints) fish stock (*you could have made the fish stock with all the trimmings of the fish you're using but that will of course be something you will have done on another occasion to keep within the tenor of this book*)

1 French loaf, slightly stale, sliced

6–7 garlic cloves, peeled

Conger Eel Chilean Style

Conger eel is a most delicious fish and even if you turn up your nose at freshwater eels, you should give conger eel a try. One of Cornwall's main exports in the Middle Ages was dried conger eel to France where it was eaten in huge quantities on days of abstinence. It's not always easy to find conger eel in fishmongers – in fact, it's not always easy to find fishmongers – but if you're in an area where there is an African or a West Indian community, it should be fairly easy to find. It is the best loved of all seafood in Chile, and this is their way of cooking it.

Preheat the oven to 150°C/300°F/gas mark 2. Heat the oil in an ovenproof casserole. Season the eel with salt and pepper, then brown lightly in the oil and remove from the pan. Add the butter and lard and fry the onions and garlic, adding the marjoram and cumin. When the onions are soft but not coloured, add the tomatoes, potatoes and the sweetcorn kernels. Stir and cover, and cook over a low heat for about 20 minutes or until the potatoes are done.

Adjust the seasoning. At this stage, add the peas or butter beans. Remove half the contents of the pan and lay the eel on top of the remainder, then return the other half to the pan to cover the fish. Cover and cook in the preheated oven for about 40 minutes or until the eel is done.

Serves 6

3 tablespoons olive or vegetable oil

1kg (2¼lb) conger eel, cut into serving collops

salt and pepper

10g (½oz) butter

10g (½oz) lard

2 medium onions, chopped

2 garlic cloves, chopped

½ teaspoon dried marjoram

½ teaspoon ground cumin

4 tomatoes, skinned and thinly sliced

4 medium potatoes, thinly sliced

2 ears of sweetcorn, kernels removed (*of course you can use tinned or frozen*)

250g (9oz) peas or butter beans (*if you're using fresh peas or butter beans, they need to be boiled first but you can use frozen peas or indeed tinned butter beans*)

Squid with Meatballs

This is a Galician dish that used to be cooked by the Spanish couple we employed, who came from that part of the world. Traditionally, it is made with large cuttlefish, but it's difficult to get cuttlefish in this country and a large squid will do just as well.

First make your meatballs. Soak the bread in the wine and squeeze it out. Then combine it with the minced meats, onion, parsley and seasoning. Roll the mixture into quite small balls, about the size of a Malteser. Dip them in the beaten egg and the flour. Heat half the olive oil in your sauté pan and fry the meatballs over a high heat until they colour, then remove them from the pan and put to one side.

Now it's time to cook the squid. Add some more oil to the pan. Crumble the stale bread and cook over a high heat until it turns golden. If you keep mashing it with your spoon it will dissolve into breadcrumbs. Fry the onion gently until it starts to soften and add the garlic and parsley. You could at this stage blend all these things if you want but if not, just leave them as they are.

Serves 4

For the meatballs

2 slices of stale bread, crusts removed

50ml (2fl oz) dry white wine

200g (7oz) lean pork, minced

200g (7oz) beef, minced

2 tablespoons finely chopped onion

1 tablespoon finely chopped parsley

salt and pepper

1 large egg, beaten

flour, for coating

125ml (4fl oz) olive oil

Sprinkle some flour into the pan with the onion mixture and cook until it turns brown. To darken the sauce (be careful not to burn it) add the tomatoes and the stock and simmer to reduce. Add the squid or cuttlefish, season and simmer for 15 minutes.

Then add the meatballs, the frozen peas and the wine and cook for some minutes longer at a simmer until the meatballs are heated through.

For the squid

1 slice of stale bread

1 onion, chopped

6 garlic cloves, finely chopped

4 tablespoons finely chopped parsley

1 tablespoon flour

100g (3½oz) tomatoes, skinned and deseeded

400ml (14fl oz) chicken stock

700g (1½lb) large squid or cuttlefish, sliced diagonally

salt and pepper

400g (14oz) frozen peas

125ml (4fl oz) dry white wine

Gigot of Monkfish with Roasted Vegetables

When I was young, monkfish was a fish that nobody wanted and nobody bought. It was largely turned into fake scampi and you could get it terribly cheaply. Now I'm afraid it is rather more expensive but a good tail of monkfish (it is never sold with the head because the head is huge and heavy and incredibly ugly as you would have seen if you were watching Jennifer and I meeting a 'monk netter' as they are appropriately called down in Mevagissey in the very first programme of *Two Fat Ladies*) is nonetheless good value. Anyway, although your gigot of monkfish may be rather costly, there is an enormous amount of very dense flesh and no bones on the monkfish and it goes very far. In fact the first dish I ever cooked on television was a tail of monkfish. This is adapted to a one-pot meal and I think is a very nice recipe.

Preheat the oven to 160°C/325°F/gas mark 3 and heat a roasting pan. Make sure that your fishmonger has skinned your monkfish because it has a variety of rather tight, muscular skins that are quite a chore to remove. Rub your monkfish with olive oil and make incisions all over it, into which you insert pieces of anchovy, garlic slices and sprigs of rosemary.

Continued overleaf

Serves 4

2kg (4lb 8oz) gigot of monkfish

150g tin anchovies in oil

2 garlic cloves, thinly sliced

branch of rosemary from which you will break sprigs

olive oil for roasting

a quantity of vegetables for roasting (*potatoes, carrots, turnips, peppers: anything you want, really; adapt the amount to how many you're feeding, and chop the vegetables into chunks about the size of the top of your thumb*)

Add enough olive oil to barely cover the base of the roasting pan and throw in all your assorted vegetables. Cook in the oven for 10 minutes, shaking the pan and turning them so that they're well coated in the oil and on their way to start roasting.

Then push the vegetables to the side of the dish and put in your prepared monkfish. Return the pan to the oven and raise the temperature to 180°C/350°F/gas mark 4 and cook for about 45 minutes or until the fish is cooked. About halfway through, cover the fish loosely with aluminium foil and check that it isn't burning. This is a most delicious dish!

Jansson's Temptation

Jansson, the son of a Swedish fisherman, became a well-known opera singer, and this dish was one that he used to cook for ladies he lured back to his flat to try to seduce. It's a very tasty dish. You should really use the Swedish anchovies, which are anchoid herring, rather than little anchovies, but if you can't get them, ordinary anchovies are fine.

Preheat the oven to 220°C/425°F/gas mark 7. Butter a gratin dish. Grate or cut your potatoes into thin strips or slices. Arrange half the potato in an even layer and put a layer of anchovies on top and then a layer of onions; continue layering the anchovies and onions, finishing with potatoes.

Press the mixture down firmly and pour the cream over the top. You may need more cream, or you might use some of the oil from the anchovy tin. Season generously with pepper and dot the top with butter.

Cook in the oven for 30 minutes, then lower the heat to 200°C/400°F/gas mark 6 for a further 30 minutes. Serve with a salad and with Swedish schnapps and cold beer.

Serves 4

900g (2lb) waxy potatoes

3 small tins anchovies or 1 large tin Swedish anchovies

3 onions, very finely sliced

275ml (3½fl oz) double cream

freshly ground black pepper

4 tablespoons butter

Wokked Prawns with Noodles

This is one of my staple dishes, and is terribly easy to make. If you don't have a wok, and indeed I don't, just use a deep sauté pan. If you leave out the noodles, you can serve the prawns as a starter.

Heat the olive oil in your wok or sauté pan and cook the ginger, garlic, spring onions, chillies and mustard seeds for a few minutes until the garlic is soft. Put in your prawns (leave the tails on if you wish) and cook until they change from transparent to opaque, turning them as you go.

Add your soya sauce and a bit of salt and throw in your noodles. Toss to heat the noodles through, and adjust the seasoning as required; perhaps more soya or salt. I add a bit of chilli sherry, and at the very last minute, when all is heated through, add your sesame oil and cook for 2–3 minutes longer.

Serves 4

olive oil

thumb-size piece of fresh ginger, peeled and cut into julienne strips

2 garlic cloves, finely chopped

6 spring onions, sliced

2 chillies, chopped

1 teaspoon mustard seeds (optional)

6 prawns per person, peeled and de-veined if necessary (use *fewer, if you're making this as a starter*)

2 teaspoons soya sauce

salt

2 packets ready-to-use noodles

dash of chilli sherry (optional)

2 teaspoons sesame oil (optional)

Moroccan Fish Stew

All along the coast of Morocco, each individual town has its own version of fish stew. To be fair, they are all much of a muchness, but each one requires (as is the way with Moroccan cooking) a sharmula, which is a marinade for the fish. This is considerably more complicated than the rest of the recipe, but well worth the effort.

Mix all the ingredients for the sharmula together and refrigerate for 1 hour before using. Marinate your fish in the sharmula for about 2 hours in a non-metallic bowl in the refrigerator.

Preheat your oven to 200°c/400°F/ gas mark 6. Oil your casserole and arrange your potatoes on the bottom. Season. Place the fish steaks on top of the potatoes and lay the green peppers and the tomato slices on top of the fish. Season again, and spoon half of the marinade over the tomato slices. Spread the tomato purée over the top of this, sprinkle with coriander and parsley and season again. Spoon the remaining sharmula over the top.

Serves 4

For the sharmula

good-sized bunch of fresh coriander, very finely chopped

good-sized bunch of fresh parsley, very finely chopped

6 garlic cloves, very finely chopped

1 small onion, very finely chopped

juice of ½ lemon

6 tablespoons olive oil

1 teaspoon freshly ground black pepper

1 teaspoon paprika

¼ teaspoon cayenne pepper

½ teaspoon freshly ground cumin seeds

¼ teaspoon ground cumin

pinch of saffron threads

salt

Cook, covered, for about 1 hour, until the fish is tender. Check after 40 minutes to see how it's getting on.

If you plan to serve with couscous and have a couscoussier, the traditional Moroccan cooking vessel, cook the stew on the hob and the couscous will steam in the top section of the pan at the same time.

For the stew

4 white fish steaks (*obviously in Morocco they use Mediterranean fish, such as swordfish or shark, but any firm white fish will do; the steaks should be about 4cm 1½ inches thick*)

1 tablespoon olive oil

2 medium potatoes, peeled and thinly sliced

salt and pepper

2 green peppers, deseeded and cut into strips

500g (18oz) ripe tomatoes, peeled, deseeded and thinly sliced

2 tablespoons tomato purée

2 tablespoons finely chopped fresh coriander

2 tablespoons finely chopped fresh parsley

Italian Mussel Stew

The Romans farmed mussels in Italy, mainly down at the Gulf of Taranto and although I prefer to eat cold water mussels, I like this recipe very much. The flavour of the chillies and tomatoes is more unusual than in the northern European recipes. I like to think of the rich ancient Roman fish aficionados lolling in their villas savouring this dish.

In a large saucepan, cook the garlic and chilli pepper in the olive oil until the garlic just begins to turn brown. This will take about 3–4 minutes. With a slotted spoon, remove the garlic and chilli and discard. Dilute the tomato purée in the water and add to the oil. Cook this for about 10 minutes, stirring from time to time.

Add all the mussels and cover tightly, shaking the casserole every now and again, and cook until the mussels are open. If any fail to open, they are not good, so throw them out. Pour in the white wine and simmer for another 7–10 minutes or so. Serve in soup bowls.

Serves 4

2 garlic cloves, finely chopped

1 dried chilli

2 tablespoons olive oil

2 tablespoons tomato purée

125ml (4fl oz) water

2kg (4lb 8oz) mussels, de-bearded and washed

225ml (8fl oz) dry white wine

Fish Stew from Syracuse

The very early food writer Archestratus, who was writing in 345 BC, came from Syracuse on the isle of Sicily. His best-known work is a poem called 'The Life of Luxury' and I like to think he might have eaten this stew. Basically, the more fish you use, the better it is and the more varied the flavours. You want to use wolf fish, hake, red snapper, monkfish, dogfish, shark, sea bass, or anything like that: good, firmish fish. Ask your fishmonger what's good and just pile it all in. It's a terribly simple stew.

Preheat the oven to 180°C/350°F/gas mark 4. Put all the ingredients in a large, deep casserole, season well, mix everything together and cook in the oven for about 45 minutes until the fish is cooked.

Serve in soup bowls with some crostini rubbed with garlic.

Serves 4

1kg (2¼lb) mixed fish fillets or steaks, cut into large chunks

1 onion, thinly sliced

2 tablespoons finely chopped parsley

3 garlic cloves, crushed

2 celery stalks, chopped

1 bay leaf

about 275g (10oz) ripe tomatoes, peeled, deseeded and chopped

5 tablespoons olive oil

225ml (8fl oz) dry white wine

850ml (1½ pints) water

salt and freshly ground black pepper

Rockfish with Plum Sauce

Claudia Roden, in her iconic book on Jewish food, refers to a recipe of the Turkish Jews, eaten on a Friday night, that she describes as rockfish with plum sauce. However, she doesn't give a recipe because she was not happy with the result. I was always intrigued by this and on finding a jar of umeboshi paste (made from pickled plums) in Waitrose, I decided to have a go with hake. So this is my variant, which probably bears no resemblance at all to the original, but I think it's rather nice.

Preheat the oven to 200°C/400°F/gas mark 6. In a pan that will hold the fish and will go into the oven, heat your olive oil and fry your onions and garlic until the onion is soft but not coloured; make sure the garlic doesn't burn. Stir in your umeboshi paste and mix well, or if using greengages or pickled plums, add them now, then stir in the sugar and the lemon juice. Season.

Put the hake into the dish, cover and cook in the oven for about 40 minutes or until the fish is done. Eat with unleavened bread or pitta bread.

Serves 4

2 tablespoons olive oil

2 onions, chopped

1 garlic clove, chopped

2 tablespoons umeboshi paste, or 6 underripe greengages, or some umeboshi plums, which you can buy in Asian shops

1 tablespoon sugar (*jaggery or palm sugar if you have it*)

juice of ½ lemon

salt and pepper

1kg (2¼lb) piece of hake

MEAT

Indonesian Grilled Beef and Vegetables

I've stretched the image of the pot a little in this recipe, using individual skewers in a grill pan. Allow 2 skewers per person.

Put all the ingredients for the marinade into a blender and pulse to a thick paste. Add a bit of salt to taste and transfer to a shallow dish. Put your cubes of meat into the mixture, turn well to coat and leave for at least 30 minutes to marinate.

Remove the meat from the marinade and thread on to skewers, alternating with the vegetables. You could use other vegetables if you wish; try sweetcorn, for instance, cut into chunks. Brush everything well with the marinade and grill for 5-8 minutes, basting with the marinade and turning several times.

Serve at once with good bread and a salad.

Serves 4

500g (18oz) rump steak or beef, cut into 2.5cm (1 inch) cubes

250g (9oz) mushrooms, halved if they are on the large side

2 sweet red peppers, deseeded and cut into 4 squares

8 shallots, peeled and halved

For the marinade

2 chillies, chopped

1 teaspoon ground coriander

½ teaspoon ground cumin

good pinch of ground turmeric

½ teaspoon dark brown sugar

¼ teaspoon shrimp paste (optional)

¼ teaspoon tamarind paste (optional)

2 garlic cloves, finely chopped

100ml (3½fl oz) thick coconut milk

salt

Steak and Kidney Pudding

This is one of the most English of dishes, and a favourite of mine on a cold winter's day. As it can be left to cook forever, it is a perfect dish to come back to if you've been out hunting or shooting. When I was at Wilde's Club, I used to make mine in a pressure cooker because it meant that I could cook them in a very short time and, given the space I had, the pressure cooker was excellent because once the pressure was up, you could take it off the heat and use the rings. And then when the pressure started going down, put it back on the stove to bring it up again.

For this recipe you will need to make a portion of suet pastry. You can buy ready-shredded suet at the shops, or you can go to the butcher's and buy some and shred it. Beef suet is not expensive to buy.

First make the pastry. Combine the flour, baking powder, suet and a pinch of salt in a mixing bowl and, using your fingers, mix it until it is the consistency of fine crumbs. Then add enough cold water to bind, mixing until the dough has a firm consistency. Knead well, then roll out three-quarters of it on a floured surface until it is the thickness required.

continued overleaf

Serves 4–6

1kg (2¼lb) stewing steak, cut into 2.5cm (1 inch) cubes (*if you're going to cook this for long enough, shin of beef is wonderful in this recipe, but otherwise use stewing steak*)

2 ox kidneys, cut into about 8 pieces (as *ox kidneys aren't always easy to get, I tend to use lambs' kidneys, in which case you'll need about 6*)

2 onions, chopped

salt and freshly ground black pepper

2 tablespoons plain flour

1 bottle brown ale

For the pastry

500g (18oz) flour

pinch of baking powder (optional)

250g (9oz) suet, finely chopped or shredded

salt and pepper

cold water

Line a 1.2 litre (2 pint) pudding basin with three-quarters of the pastry, leaving an overlap to seal it afterwards. Then put in the mixture of steak, kidney and onions, and season with salt and pepper and stir in a little plain flour to help thicken the gravy. (You can if you like add oysters or mushrooms to this dish, but I prefer not to.) Then pour in your ale so that it comes within 5cm (2 inches) of the top of the basin.

Roll out the remainder of the pastry to form a lid. Moisten the edges of the pastry with water and cover the pudding with the pastry lid, and press together firmly so that nothing escapes. Then turn up the overhanging pieces of pastry. Wrap your pastry basin in a tea-towel which you have soaked in hot water and wrung out well and then tie up the pudding with string which will act as a handle to take it in and out of the boiling water.

Put the pudding basin in a large pan of boiling water and let it boil for at least 4 hours. Replenish the water, if necessary, from a jug – but do not let the pudding stop boiling. This dish can cook quite happily for up to 8 hours without being overcooked.

Remove the cloth and send the pudding to the table in the basin. If you don't like the look of your pudding basin, pin a napkin round it. I think it constitutes a whole meal, but if you would like some greens too, and as you are steaming, put some chopped cabbage in a colander and steam this on top of the pudding for the last 20 minutes or so.

Dfeena

This is an Egyptian dish that I first came across with my father's medical colleague, Dr Halim Grace, who gave my mother a recipe for it. The eggs are cooked whole in their shells and have a very interesting and creamy flavour about them. I have to say that I have leaned heavily on Claudia Roden's recipe in *A Book of Middle Eastern Food* for my version of this, but I hope you will try it; it's a very interesting dish and of course a one-pot meal.

Preheat the oven to 190°C/375°F/gas mark 5. Put the meat, eggs and all the vegetables and spices in a large oven-proof pot or casserole with a tight-fitting lid. Pour on some water until the contents are barely covered and season.

Cover the pot and cook in the oven for 1 hour, then lower the temperature to the lowest possible setting and let it continue to simmer for at least 4 hours, or overnight if you like. The stew can be cooked on top of the stove but it's better to cook it in the oven. Claudia Roden suggests that you add a calf's foot, but they're not easy to come by. I have added a pig's trotter on occasion, which adds an extra richness to the sauce.

I think you'll enjoy this because it's lovely to sit round the Aga in a warm winter kitchen and eat with gusto. This dish fits the bill perfectly, especially as everyone has to peel their own eggs!

Serves 6

- 1kg (2¼lb) stewing beef, cut into cubes
- 6 eggs, in their shells
- 2 large onions, finely chopped
- 3–4 carrots, depending on size, chopped
- 3 large potatoes, peeled and chopped into pieces, or quartered small potatoes
- 300g (10½oz) chickpeas (*if these are dried, soak them overnight, but I tend to use tinned*)
- 2 garlic cloves, crushed
- 1 teaspoon ground allspice
- 1 teaspoon ground cumin
- salt and freshly ground black pepper

Stuffed Vegetable Marrow

I'm a great devotee of stuffed marrow, and had been racking my brains how to make it a one-pot meal when a friend of mine said that she always cooked the marrow in the pan in which she had cooked the stuffing, so that solved that. And in fact if you add a little water to the pan, you'll get a nice gravy to boot. I had some argument with myself, and indeed others, as to whether a vegetable marrow constituted a one-pot meal if you didn't add extra vegetables, so I came up with a solution that you stuffed one half with the meat stuffing and the other half with the vegetable stuffing. I don't usually do this at home, regarding the marrow as being the vegetable.

Preheat the oven to 200°C/400°F/gas mark 6. In a pan big enough to fit your marrow and that will go into the oven and on the hob, fry your onion and garlic and green pepper in the oil until the onion is soft. Add your mince and season with pepper. Once the mince is brown, pour in your tin of tomatoes and tomato purée, stir well and cook for about 5 minutes longer. Add salt to taste.

In the meantime, cut the marrow in half lengthways and scoop out the seeds, which will give you a nice indentation in the middle. Fill the middle in one half with your cooked mince. Throw all the vegetables for the stuffing together with the pickled lemon into the pan from which you have removed the mince and cook for a few minutes. Season. Then stuff the other side of the marrow. Put the mince half on top of the vegetable half and wrap in aluminium foil.

continued overleaf

Serves 4

2 small onions, finely chopped

1 garlic clove, chopped

1 green pepper, deseeded and finely chopped

1 tablespoon olive oil

450g (1lb) butcher's mince (*don't buy that slimy stuff you get in supermarkets*)

salt and pepper

400g (14oz) tin tomatoes

1 tablespoon tomato purée

1 good-sized vegetable marrow

For the vegetable stuffing

4–5 young runner beans

5–6 mushrooms, chopped

1 potato, diced

½ pickled lemon, if you have it, or the juice and rind of 1 lemon

salt and pepper

Place the marrow in your sauté pan and pour enough water into the pan to come about a third of the way up the marrow. Cook in the preheated oven or, if necessary, on top of the stove with the lid on for about 1 hour or until the marrow is done. Clearly, the cooking time will be dictated by the size of the marrow.

Unwrap the marrow, cut into thick slices and serve with crusty bread.

Beef Cobbler

A cobbler is a dish that is topped with scone dough. It is now used extensively in America, both for sweet and savoury cobblers and it was a dish that probably would have gone out with the Pilgrim Fathers. It's one that was rather a loss to us in this country, where it is now relatively uncommon.

Preheat the oven to 180°C/350°F/gas mark 4.

Mix all the scone ingredients, except the beaten egg, to make a smooth dough, adding your liquid rather circumspectly so that the dough doesn't become too liquid.

Cut the meat into cubes and toss in the seasoned flour. In a heavy casserole, fry the meat, onion, carrots and celery until the meat is brown and the onion is soft and pale gold. Stir in any remaining flour and add the stock and the ale, together with the walnuts. Bring this to the boil and cook in the preheated oven for 2 hours.

Shape the scone mixture into 8 rounds and place on top of the meat, leaving a gap in the middle, and glaze with the beaten egg. Return to the oven and cook for a further 20–25 minutes until the scones are brown.

Serves 4

1kg (2¼lb) stewing beef

40g (1½oz) seasoned flour

1 onion, sliced

225g (8oz) carrots, sliced

50g (2oz) celery, chopped

700ml (1¼ pints) brown stock

150ml (5fl oz) brown ale

handful of walnuts, or 4–5 pickled walnuts

For the scone dough

500g (18oz) self-raising flour (*You can use plain flour if you prefer, in which case you'll need to add ½ teaspoon baking powder*)

1 teaspoon salt

110g (4oz) butter

110g (4oz) sugar

2 eggs

150ml (5fl oz) milk

1 egg, beaten

Brisket of Beef

My friend Jan McCourt of Northfield Farm in Rutland produces the most immaculate meat and his brisket, an inexpensive cut of meat from the breast, is particularly good. Once again, this is a dish that is very good for cooking in the Aga, if you happen to have one.

Smother the meat in the seasoned flour. Melt the dripping in the pan and brown the beef, then remove while you fry the bacon, onions, carrots, celery and potatoes, until the onions are soft. Pour the ale over the vegetables. Add the sugar, salt and pepper and return the meat to the pan on top of the vegetables. Cover and cook over a low heat or in a slow oven, 160°C/325°F/gas mark 3, if you prefer, for 2½ hours.

Remove the meat and vegetables to a serving dish, then reduce the cooking liquid over a high heat and pour it around the meat.

Serves 4

1kg (2¼lb) brisket of beef, boned and rolled (*ask your butcher to do this for you*)

40g (1½oz) flour, seasoned with salt, pepper, dried mustard and cayenne pepper

30g (1¼oz) beef dripping (*or use cooking oil*)

125g (4½oz) streaky bacon, chopped

4 onions, chopped

3–4 carrots, chopped

2 celery stalks, chopped

3 potatoes, cut into smallish pieces

300ml (10fl oz) brown ale

2 teaspoons brown sugar

salt and pepper

Filipino Beef Stew Called Carri Carri

This is a very filling dish, which tends to be eaten as a Sunday or holiday lunch so you can go to sleep afterwards. Every Filipino cook has a version of this dish in their repertoire. You may not be able to get the annatto seeds or powder that give the dish its unusual colouring, but it doesn't really matter other than for authenticity. It's a very economical recipe, using either oxtail or shin of beef.

Trim the excess fat off the meat. In a large, heavy pan, heat the oil and brown the meat in batches. Transfer it to a plate and fry the annatto seeds (if using) in the remaining fat. Keep them covered to prevent them popping out because they do jump around quite a lot. The oil will then become a bright orange colour. Remove the pan from the heat and discard the seeds.

Add the onions and garlic to the oil and cook, stirring occasionally, until soft. Return the meat to the pan and add the water and pepper. Bring this to the boil, then cover the pan and reduce to a simmer over a low heat until the meat is tender. When you turn down the heat, add your salt. The stew will probably need about 2 hours' cooking. If you want, you can leave it overnight which means you can skim off any excess fat once it has cooled.

Serves 6

2.5kg (5lb 8oz) oxtail or shin of beef, cut through the bone

3 tablespoons oil

2 tablespoons annatto seeds or 1 tablespoon annatto powder (*if you can get them*)

2 large onions, sliced

1–2 garlic cloves, depending on their size, finely chopped

2 litres (3½ pints) water

good grinding of black pepper

3 teaspoons salt

4 tablespoons roasted and ground rice (*you can buy this in Asian shops*)

4 tablespoons crushed, roasted peanuts

250g (9oz) green beans (*I use runner beans for this quite often*)

Mix the ground rice and peanuts together, and top and tail the beans, cutting them into small pieces. Cut your aubergine into thick, diagonal slices. Add all this to the pan with the beef mixture and stir gently, simmering until the vegetables are tender and the sauce has thickened, which should take about 30 minutes. Add the fish sauce and taste to see if you need more. Stir in the sliced spring onions and the celery leaves and cook for a further 10 minutes or so.

I tend to eat this stew with Asian breads, but if you want to have potatoes, you could add them to the stew just before you add the other vegetables. Use small new potatoes, or larger ones cut into pices, and cook until ready to serve.

200g (7oz) aubergine, sliced
(*or the nice little ones you can get in Asian shops in which case just split in half*)

1 dessertspoon fish sauce

3 spring onions, sliced crossways

3 tablespoons celery leaves
(*or you can use celery salt*)

Lamb Boulangère

This French dish translates as 'baker's wife lamb'. This was no doubt reference to the fact that in the days before people had ovens in their houses, they would take their dish to the bakery. Once the baker had removed the bread from the oven, he would replace it with people's dishes which they would later come and collect, and presumably paying a small fee for the privilege. The size of the leg of lamb determines exactly how many it will feed.

Preheat your oven to 220°c/425°F/gas mark 7. Make small incisions all over the lamb and stick the garlic and rosemary into the slits. Place two tablespoons of water in a shallow, earthenware dish and put in the lamb. Season it and dot with half the butter. Roast the lamb in the hot oven for 20 minutes, basting from time to time.

Remove the dish from the oven and transfer the lamb to a plate. Mix together the potatoes, onion, garlic, bay leaf and thyme and season. Put the potato mixture into the baking dish and pour on enough boiling salted water to reach the height of the potatoes. Cook over a medium heat on the hob until the water returns to the boil. Then lay the lamb on top of the potatoes and dot with the remaining butter.

Return the dish to the oven and roast for at least another 20 minutes, turning the leg of lamb during the course of the cooking. The potatoes should then be ready, but continue to cook until the lamb is done to your liking. The French eat it pink but you may prefer it a little more well-done. Serve.

Serves 6–8

1 leg of lamb (*smallish, unless you're having a big party*)

3 garlic cloves, cut into slivers

3 sprigs of rosemary

salt and pepper

60g (2½oz) butter

1kg (2¼lb) potatoes, very thinly sliced

1 onion, very thinly sliced

1 garlic clove, chopped

1 bay leaf

2 sprigs of thyme

Lamb with Pumpkin and Mint

This is an Armenian dish and can be served either with steamed bulgur wheat or with couscous which takes virtually no cooking. The dish is traditionally made with lamb shanks. I'm slightly off lamb shanks, which I never really thought were a particularly good cut of the meat; and then they've become fashionable and I do hate things that are fashionable. But use lamb shanks if you have them, otherwise use shoulder of lamb, cut through the bone into pieces.

Preheat the oven to 160°C/325°F/gas mark 3. Heat the olive oil in a large pot and brown the lamb on all sides over a medium heat. It doesn't need to be heavily browned. Throw in the garlic and season. Pour in the water and bring this to the boil, removing any scum that rises to the top. Add the tomatoes and lemon juice and simmer either on top of the stove or in the preheated oven for 1½ hours until the meat is tender.

Add the pumpkin and green pepper, bring to the boil and then reduce the heat and simmer for 1 hour, until the pumpkin is tender. Adjust the seasoning, add more lemon juice if liked, and then add the mint and cook for another minute or two before serving.

Serves 6

1 tablespoon olive oil

1.5kg (3lb 5oz) lamb shoulder or shanks

2 garlic cloves, finely chopped

salt and pepper

1.5 litres (2½ pints) water

3-4 chopped tomatoes

4 tablespoons lemon juice

1–1.5kg (2¼ –3lb 5oz) pumpkin, peeled, deseeded and cut into 5cm (2 inch) pieces

1 sweet green pepper, deseeded and cut into 2.5cm (1 inch) squares

4 tablespoons chopped fresh mint leaves

2 tablespoons crushed dried mint leaves

Spring Lamb with Lettuce Leaves

I can't remember where I first came across this Turkish dish. I've made a note in the margin of my notebook that the original dish had carrots in it, but as I'm known for disliking carrots, I've removed them and substituted aubergine and I think it works very well.

Melt your butter in the base of a heavy pan and spread the spring onions, aubergine and onion pieces over. Scatter the shredded lettuce evenly on top of the vegetables; it might look a lot but the lettuce will diminish as it cooks. Rub the chunks of lamb with lemon and place them on the lettuce. Add the sugar, a little salt and pepper and the water.

Cover and cook on a very low heat for 2½–3 hours, until the meat is tender and the water has reduced by about half. Add the dill and cook for 5 minutes or so more.

Serves 4

30g (1¼oz) butter

3 bunches of spring onions, cut into 5cm (2 inch) lengths

3–4 aubergines, depending on size, thinly sliced

1 onion, cut into 8 pieces

2 large round lettuce, roughly shredded

2 large cos lettuce, roughly shredded

3kg (6lb 8oz) leg of spring lamb on the bone, cut into chunks

½ lemon

½ teaspoon sugar

salt and pepper

250ml (9fl oz) water

4 tablespoons chopped dill

Lamb Curry

I love lamb curry. When you eat it in India, however, it is as likely to be mutton or hogget (a yearling) as lamb. It really doesn't matter, it's just a question of timing, although the mutton obviously has more flavour. I'm also giving you a recipe for Kashmiri garam masala because you can make it in advance and have it ready for when you come to cook the curry. And, of course, you can use it in any other curry you like.

In a heavy pan, roast separately the cumin seeds, the cardamom pods, the nigella seeds and the cinnamon sticks broken into pieces. Turn each of them on to a plate to cool. Put them in your grinder and grind into a fine powder. Combine with the ground cloves, mace and nutmeg and store in an airtight jar. My mother's mixture kept for all the years I can remember.

Cut your lamb or mutton into cubes. Heat the ghee in a heavy pan and fry the onions, garlic and ginger over a low heat until soft and golden. Sprinkle in the curry powder, salt and vinegar. Stir thoroughly. Add the lamb or mutton and cook, stirring constantly, until everything is coated with the spice mixture.

continued on page 144

Serves 6–8

For the Kashmiri garam masala

1 tablespoon cumin seeds

2 teaspoons black cumin seeds

1 tablespoon small green cardamom pods

1 teaspoon nigella seeds (*if you don't have these you can use fennel seeds*)

2 cinnamon sticks

1 teaspoon ground cloves

2 teaspoons ground mace

1 whole nutmeg, finely grated

For the curry

1.5kg (3lb 5oz) boned shoulder of lamb or mutton

2 tablespoons ghee or oil

2 large onions, chopped

1 tablespoon chopped garlic

1 tablespoon peeled and finely chopped fresh ginger

1 teaspoon curry powder

2 teaspoons salt

Add the tomatoes, chillies and mint, cover and cook over a low heat, until the meat is tender – probably about 1 hour. If it appears to be drying out, add a little hot water to prevent it sticking. Five minutes before the end, add the garam masala and some fresh coriander or mint leaves if you like. You can eat this with parathas or chapattis or nan bread. Enjoy it!

2 tablespoons vinegar or lemon juice

3 large tomatoes, skinned and chopped

2 fresh chillies, sliced

2 tablespoons chopped fresh mint leaves

1 teaspoon garam masala

fresh coriander or mint leaves, to garnish (optional)

Slow-cooked Lamb with Tomatoes and Beans

This is a dish that's perfect for cooking in an Aga and is incredibly easy. You take either the shoulder or a small leg of lamb, throw everything else in with it and just let it cook; the vegetables and the tomatoes in the dish make the sauce.

Preheat the oven to 160°C/325°F/gas mark 3. Put your cumin seeds into a roasting pan and cook over the heat until the cumin seeds pop. This is an optional extra but it does give a stronger flavour to the cumin. Place the lamb in the pan, surround with the sliced onion and just add everything else. As you are using anchovies you won't need salt, but give it a good grinding of black pepper.

Cook this in the second oven of the Aga or in the preheated oven for 2 hours or more. You can, if you want, add small new potatoes, cut in half, for the last hour, although I tend to mop up my juices with bread.

Serves 4

1 teaspoon cumin seeds

1 shoulder of lamb, boned if you can get your butcher to do it

2 onions, sliced

2 × 400g (14oz) tins tomatoes

2 × 400g (14oz) tins haricot beans, drained (*if you are using fresh haricot beans, you will need to soak these for several hours before you use them but the tinned ones are fine*)

2 garlic cloves

50g tin anchovy fillets in oil

150ml (5fl oz) red wine (*or rosé will do perfectly well if you happen to be following the current fashion*)

freshly ground black pepper

Bolton Hot Pot

This is a variant on Lancashire hot pot. Its peculiarity is that it contains the black pudding for which Bolton is famous, and lambs' kidneys as opposed to the oysters of Lancashire hot pot. Although you can add oysters as well if you want. It's a very good dish and doesn't need to be cooked in the tall pot that was used for the original hot pot.

Preheat the oven to 160°C/325°F/gas mark 3. Heat the lard in a casserole and brown the lamb pieces on all sides. Remove these with a slotted spoon and set aside. Fry the onion in the same fat until it is pale gold, then stir in the flour and let it brown. Add the stock slowly, stirring all the time to make a smooth gravy. Season and add a pinch of sugar.

Return the lamb pieces to the pan and put a layer of kidneys over them and then the mushrooms in a layer. Season well with pepper and salt. Put the potatoes on top, overlapping them like scales. Dot the top with butter or dripping to keep the potatoes moist. Cover and cook in the oven for 2 hours. After 1½ hours remove the top to let the potatoes brown.

Serves 4

30g (1¼oz) lard or dripping

1kg (2¼lb) best end of neck of lamb, cut into pieces and the fat trimmed

1 onion, quite thickly sliced

30g (1¼oz) flour

450ml (15fl oz) meat stock

salt and pepper

pinch of sugar

4 lambs' kidneys, skinned, cored and sliced

125g (4½oz) mushrooms, quartered

1kg (2¼lb) potatoes, thinly sliced

20g (¾oz) butter or dripping

Romanian Pork

When I was turning out my parents' house, I came across a cutting my mother had kept, about somebody who had won a cookery competition with this recipe. The woman in question was a Romanian and I rather liked the recipe, so I copied it out before I ever thought to be cooking for a living. Sadly, I copied only the recipe and not the name of the person who won the prize. Over the years I've made certain changes, but it's still, I think, a very good dish.

Rub the meat with the salt and pepper, add the cumin, then place in an earthenware dish and leave in a cool place for at least 4 hours. Mix the chopped vegetables, seasonings, wine and vinegar together and pour this over the meat in the dish. Leave it once more, turning the meat from time to time, for about 2 hours.

Preheat your oven to 190°C/375°F/gas mark 5. Remove the meat from the marinade, pat it dry, then put it in an ovenproof casserole and roast it for 25 minutes, turning it once. Pour over the juices and the vegetables and cook for 1 hour, basting occasionally. If it becomes too dry, add a little water.

Remove the meat and vegetables from the pan and arrange on a hot serving plate. Mix the sour cream with the cornflour and stir this into the juices. Simmer over a low heat, stirring until it is smooth and thick, and correct the seasoning. Slice the meat and pour the sauce over the meat and vegetables.

Serves 6–8

1.5kg (3lb 5oz) shoulder of pork, boned and rolled (*you can use leg instead, but it's a bit of a waste to use loin*)

salt and pepper

½ teaspoon ground cumin

1 large onion, roughly chopped

2 carrots, roughly chopped

2 celery stalks, roughly chopped

2 garlic cloves, roughly chopped

1 bay leaf

½ teaspoon thyme

salt

6–8 peppercorns

200ml (7fl oz) dry white wine

100ml (3½fl oz) wine vinegar

3 tablespoons sour cream

½ teaspoon cornflour

Cassoeula

This is a dish from the Brianza region of northern Italy. It's a real rib-sticker and quite delicious. If you get the opportunity, obtain a pig's trotter and cut it into 4 pieces. Without it, the finished dish will not be quite so perfect.

In a large pot, soften the onions and the butter over a medium heat. Add the pork rind and the trotter and brown lightly. Pour over enough water to cover, and simmer, partly covered, for 1 hour, turning occasionally to prevent sticking.

When the water has nearly all evaporated, add the ribs, cook for about 15 minutes, then add the carrots, celery and cabbage and cook for a further 30 minutes. Then add the sausages. At this stage you can stir in a little tomato purée if you like.

Cook for another 30 minutes or until the cabbage is tender, correct the seasoning and serve. Good country bread goes particularly well with this.

Serves 4

4 small onions, sliced

200g (7oz) butter

125g (4½oz) pork rind, cut into strips

1 pig's trotter

700g (1½lb) pork spare ribs, cut into sections

4 carrots, sliced

1 celery stalk, sliced

1 large cabbage, coarsely shredded

300g (10½oz) small, spicy cooking sausages

1 teaspoon tomato purée (optional)

salt and pepper

Roast Pork with Provençal Vegetables and Potatoes

I have never really understood why the French remove the rind from their pork before cooking, thus losing the joys of crackling. The same is found in Scottish cooking, so it may be that historically the pigs never fattened sufficiently to produce proper crackling. The rind is usually cut into small pieces and added to the dish, or where it is not used it is kept for another day.

Make incisions in the pork and insert the sage leaves and the garlic slivers. Mix the salt with the thyme and the bay leaf and coat the pork with this mixture. Leave to marinate for several hours or overnight at room temperature.

Preheat the oven to 180°C/350°F/gas mark 4. Throw out any liquid that has come from the pork and wipe off the excess salt. Tie up the roast if necessary and put it in an ovenproof dish. Cover with the lard or olive oil and place in the oven for 20 minutes.

Remove the meat and put all the vegetables and bouquet garni into the ovenproof dish and sauté them in 4 tablespoons olive oil on top of the hob for a few minutes. Then return the pork to the pan on top of the vegetables and continue to roast, basting from time to time, for another 45 minutes to 1 hour.

Serves 4–6

1kg (2¼lb) boned pork, rind removed

12 large sage leaves

1 garlic clove, thinly sliced

2 teaspoons salt

1 teaspoon thyme

1 bay leaf

20g (¾oz) lard, thinly sliced, or 1 tablespoon olive oil

2 aubergines, peeled and cut into large cubes

4 tomatoes, cut into quarters

500g (18oz) potatoes, peeled and thinly sliced

3 onions, thinly sliced

1 bouquet garni

4 tablespoons olive oil

Pork and Chestnut Casserole

This is a basic stew to which you can add all sorts of ingredients - whatever comes to mind - but this will give you the general idea.

Put all the marinade ingredients in a bowl, add the meat and leave overnight at room temperature. The next day, strain the marinade through a colander and reserve the liquid. Remove the meat from the colander and dry on kitchen paper. Season with salt and pepper.

Preheat the oven to 160°c/325°F/gas mark 3. Melt some lard or oil in a large sauté pan and brown the meat for 15-20 minutes, turning the pieces as they cook. Return the marinade to the pan with the extra onions and cook for 50 minutes, either in a low oven or on top of the stove.

After about 40 minutes, add the chestnuts and mushrooms (if using) at this stage. I do think the flavours of chestnuts and mushrooms marry together particularly well. Replace the lid on the casserole and leave to cook for a further hour.

Serves 4

500g (18oz) lean, boneless pork, cut into cubes

salt and pepper

lard or oil, for frying

3 onions, sliced

1 packet of chestnuts, ready peeled (*vacuum-packed are easiest, I find*)

110g (4oz) mushrooms (optional)

For the marinade

2 onions, sliced

½ bottle red wine

bunch of parsley, chopped

several sprigs of thyme, crumbled

3 garlic cloves, crushed

1 bay leaf

Alsatian Sauerkraut

There are all sorts of ways of cooking pork with sauer-kraut, whatever country you're looking at. This is one I particularly like. It uses smoked pork ribs and it should have smoked sausage, but I tend to use frankfurters, despite the fact that it's now easier to buy smoked sausage here. As an alternative, Polish boiling sausages will do very well.

In a heavy-based pan, sauté the onion in the fat until it is golden. Add the sauerkraut, unwashed or briefly rinsed, and cook for 5 minutes longer, stirring with a fork. Add the wine, apple and crushed juniper berries. Pour in enough stock to cover the sauerkraut and put in the piece of salted or smoked ribs. Cook over a low heat for 2–3 hours. One hour before serving add the bacon in a piece and the saus-ages. Forty-five minutes before serving add the potatoes. Thirty minutes before serving add the Kirsch.

When ready to serve, remove the pork ribs and the bacon and slice them. Arrange the sauerkraut on a dish and heap the bacon, pork and sausages on top of it with the potatoes.

Serves 4

1 onion, finely chopped

2–3 tablespoons goose fat or lard

500g (18oz) sauerkraut

250ml (9fl oz) white wine

1 apple, halved, cored and diced

12 juniper berries, crushed, then tied up in a piece of muslin

200ml (7fl oz) stock

500g (18oz) salted pork ribs or smoked pork ribs, in a piece

500g (18oz) smoked streaky bacon, in a piece

6 frankfurters or the equivalent in smoked sausage

6 small potatoes, in their skins

2 tablespoons Kirsch

Lentils with Merguez Sausages

In order to stay within the spirit of this book, you must make this dish with a jar or tin of lentils, or when you have some leftover cooked lentils. This recipe is adapted from one in Annie Bell's excellent book *Evergreen*, now sadly out of print, for a vegetarian dish that she serves with Colcannon, a traditional Irish dish of potatoes and cabbage.

Soak the mushrooms in 150ml (5fl oz) boiling water for 15 minutes.

Put all the ingredients, including the liquid from the mushrooms, into a pan, bring to the boil, cover and simmer for 40 minutes.

Serves 4

7g dried wild mushrooms

250g (9oz) cooked brown lentils

4 merguez or other spicy sausages

450g (1lb) shallots, peeled and left whole

175g (6oz) baby carrots, washed, topped and tailed

several sprigs of thyme

1 bay leaf

1½ glasses red wine

1 tablespoon olive oil

salt and pepper

Sausage Casserole

A sausage casserole is an excellent and cheap way of entertaining your friends. You will need good sausages but it's quite nice if you use ordinary sausages inter-mingled with some of the spicy Italian or French Toulouse sausages that you can find on the market. This dish is about as simple as you can get, and if you turn the oven down, you can go away and leave it. Normally I would serve it with mash, but for the purposes of this book I would suggest that you add either very small potatoes or chopped potatoes to the casserole and let them all cook together.

Preheat the oven to 180°C/350°F/gas mark 4. In a heavy casserole, fry the onions in the oil until they are coloured. Add the garlic and cook a little longer. Brown the sausages in the pan and then pour in the tomatoes and whatever alcohol you're using.

Season, add your potatoes and cook gently, covered, in the preheated oven for about 1 hour. Some 10 minutes before the end, open the casserole, sprinkle on the grated Cheddar and cook for the remaining time with the lid off. Alternatively, put it under the grill to brown.

Serves 4

4 onions, sliced

1 tablespoon oil

2 garlic cloves, crushed

900g (2lb) mixed sausages

400g (14oz) tin chopped tomatoes

½ bottle red wine or 1 bottle beer

salt and pepper

6 medium potatoes, cut in half

75g (3oz) Cheddar cheese, grated

Pork with Clams

This is a much-loved Portuguese dish, and although it sounds very unlikely, it's the most excellent example of surf and turf.

Crush your garlic and salt together with a pestle and mortar. Brush the meat with this paste and then sprinkle the piri-piri sauce over the top of it. Cover and refrigerate for 24 hours.

Cut the meat into squares. Wash the clams thoroughly in several changes of water. Fry the meat in the lard for 10 minutes or so until it is brown. Then add the clams and cook over a high heat so that they open quickly. Discard any that don't open and serve at once with bread and a nice tomato and onion salad.

Serves 4

4 garlic cloves

2 teaspoons salt

750g (1lb 10oz) loin of pork

2 tablespoons piri-piri sauce

900g (2lb) clams

4 tablespoons lard

Pork Loaf en Croûte

This is a recipe that for a number of years I have used simply to make a pork and egg pie, but with shortcrust pastry rather than hot-water dough. When I was mulling over one-pot ideas it struck me that I could replace some of the eggs with leeks or some other vegetable and turn this into a perfect one-pot dish because it's made in a roll.

Preheat the oven to 170°C/325°F/gas mark 3. Roll out a third of your pastry thinly in a rectangular shape and lay it on a greased baking tray. Combine your onion and parsley and mix them in with the minced pork. Then take half of the minced pork and set it on to your rectangular pastry, leaving a 2cm (¾ inch) border all round.

Make a trough in the middle along the length of the meat and arrange your eggs, chicory, gherkins and anything else that may take your fancy in this trough. Season with salt and pepper and cover with the rest of the pork. Smooth this with a knife that you've dipped into hot water.

Roll out the rest of the pastry so that it is actually 8cm (3 inches) larger than the base. Wind it round the rolling pin and unroll it over the meat. Press it into place around the meat and crimp it with a knife. Then glaze it with egg or milk. Cut a slit in the centre of the pastry to allow the steam to escape and decorate the pastry if you wish, with criss-cross patterns or whatever you like.

Bake in the oven for 45 minutes, then cover the pie with a little aluminium foil to prevent the crust from burning and bake for another 45 minutes. Serve directly from the baking tray.

Serves 4

either 1 portion of shortcrust pastry or 1 packet of puff pastry (*you can of course buy your shortcrust pastry*)

1 onion, finely chopped

2 tablespoons finely chopped parsley

450g (1lb) minced pork

3 hard-boiled eggs

2 heads of chicory (*I originally used leeks but these need to be blanched first so I substituted chicory and that worked very well*)

2–3 gherkins

salt and pepper

egg or milk, to glaze

Puerto Rican Rice

One of the most enjoyable and entertaining books I have read in recent times is called *The Hungry Cyclist* by Tom Kevill-Davies, a young man who cycled up one side of North America and down the other, and then through Central and into South America, finishing up in Rio de Janeiro, with a view to eating his way round America and finding local dishes. One of the earliest dishes in the book is when he's confronted by a group of less-than-safe Puerto Ricans who welcome him into their midst and feed him. This is what they gave him and he's very gracefully and graciously allowed me to use the recipe.

In a small pot, bring the peas and 700ml (1¼ pints) water to the boil, turn off the heat, cover and allow to stand for 1 hour, then drain. However, in the interests of one-pot cooking, I'd use tinned haricot beans instead.

In a deep pan, sauté the salt pork, onion and garlic in the olive oil for a few minutes. Add the peppers, cover and cook until the onion begins to turn translucent. Add the tomatoes, drained peas or beans and the stock and simmer, covered, over a low heat for 15 minutes until the peas are almost tender and most of the liquid is absorbed.

Stir in the annatto oil, rice, black pepper and 500ml (18fl oz) cold water. Return to the boil, then simmer, covered, for 15–20 minutes until the liquid is absorbed and the rice is soft and tender. Season to taste and mix in the coriander and chilli garnishes and squeeze over the lime juice.

Serves 4

200g (7oz) dried pigeon peas or black-eyed peas; or 400g (14oz) tin haricot beans

100g (3½) salt pork or bacon, chopped into small pieces

1 small onion, chopped

2 garlic cloves, crushed

1 tablespoon olive oil

1 red pepper, deseeded and chopped into small pieces

1 green pepper, deseeded and chopped into small pieces

2 tomatoes, chopped

250ml (9fl oz) chicken or ham stock

1 tablespoon annatto oil (*if you don't have this, use any oil*)

200g (7oz) long-grain rice

salt and freshly ground black pepper

To garnish

handful of coriander leaves

3 chillies, chopped

juice of 3 limes

VEGETARIAN

Gratin of Chicory and Spinach

This gratin is particularly nice and soothing. Don't forget when cleaning the chicory to cut out the core at the base, which is the really bitter part of it.

Preheat the oven to 190°C/375°F/gas mark 5. Oil a large gratin dish with 1 tablespoon olive oil. Combine the chicory and spinach in the dish and season. Mix together the breadcrumbs and cheeses and sprinkle on top, then dribble the remaining oil over the surface.

Cook in the oven for about 45 minutes. If it is not brown enough already, flash it under the grill for a few minutes.

Serves 4

4 tablespoons olive oil

1kg (2¼lb) chicory, trimmed and each head cut into 4

1kg (2¼lb) spinach, stems removed, finely chopped

salt and pepper

4 tablespoons dried breadcrumbs

30g (1¼oz) Parmesan cheese, grated

100g (3½oz) hard cheese, grated (*I would use Cheddar for this but Cheshire is also good*)

Tarte of Herbs

This is a recipe from John Evelyn's *Acetaria*, published in 1699, and at that time all green leafy vegetables were known as herbs. It is an excellent, delicious tart and I recommend it to you even though it's three centuries old. The combination of sweet and savoury flavours so beloved in the Middle Ages left our tables over the course of the seventeenth and eighteenth centuries, so this is one of the last examples in English cookery.

Preheat the oven to 220°C/425°F/gas mark 7. Put a baking sheet in the oven to heat up so your pastry won't get a soggy bottom. Wash the spinach, chard and chervil in hot water. Drain them well and chop. Mix the cream with the breadcrumbs and add the chopped herbs, then add the ground almonds or macaroon crumbs, the butter and the beaten eggs. Finally add the currants, salt, sugar and nutmeg. Stir it all together.

Line a 22.5cm (9 inch) flan tin with the rolled-out pastry and pour in the herb mixture. Bake on the hot baking sheet in the preheated oven for 10 minutes. Then lower the temperature to 180°C/350°F/gas mark 4 and cook the tart for a further 30–40 minutes until it is nicely set. Serve hot or warm.

Serves 6–8

500g (18oz) spinach

250g (9oz) chard

60g (2½oz) chervil

300ml (10fl oz) double cream

30g (1¼oz) fresh breadcrumbs

30g (1¼oz) ground almonds or macaroon crumbs

60g (2½oz) butter

2 eggs plus 2 egg yolks, beaten

60g (2½oz) currants

salt

3 tablespoons sugar

good grating of nutmeg

1 packet of puff pastry

Bitter Melon Curry

It can be difficult to find vegetables for vegetarian dishes that will keep their texture for any length of time. One of the best is the bitter melon, a type of gourd that you will see in Asian shops, looking rather like a scaly ant-eater and somewhat prehistoric. It should be bought young and dark green, in which case you can use the whole vegetable. If it is paler, the seeds will be hard and need to be discarded. But it is an excellent vegetable for adding to all sorts of dishes. An Irish potato is what we think of as an ordinary potato.

Slice the bitter melons across on the slant, to a thickness of about 6mm (¼ inch). Rub 1 teaspoon salt and the turmeric over the cut surfaces. Peel and dice the potatoes. Cut the beans into bite-size pieces, and de-string them if necessary. Cut the broccoli stem into thick slices and divide the florets, leaving a small stem on each.

In a heavy pan, heat the oil or ghee and fry the bitter melon slices until they are golden brown on both sides, then remove on to kitchen paper to drain. Put the mustard seeds into the pan and cook them until they pop. Then add the ginger and chilli and continue to cook, stirring, until the ginger is soft. Add all the vegetables and cook for another 10 minutes. Season with salt, add the sugar and about 150ml (5fl oz) hot water.

Cover and cook over a very slow heat until the vegetables are tender. This should take about 15 minutes. About half-way through this, add the fried bitter melon to the pan. Once the vegetables are ready, turn off the heat and stir the mustard into the liquid evenly. This dish can be prepared ahead of time and reheated. Serve with Asian bread.

Serves 4

2 medium-sized bitter melons

salt

½ teaspoon ground turmeric

1 medium sweet potato

1 large Irish potato

about 10 young runner beans

1 medium-sized broccoli head

3 tablespoons vegetable oil or ghee (*if you have it*)

1 teaspoon mustard seeds

1 tablespoon peeled and finely grated fresh ginger

1 tablespoon sliced fresh chilli

2 teaspoons jaggery (palm) sugar or brown sugar

1 teaspoon mild English mustard

Broccoli in the Sicilian Style

I found this recipe in an old book called *The Good and True Cooking of Italy,* and I think it works really well. The anchovy fillets, although not strictly vegetarian, give an extra depth of flavour.

Cover the base of a large sauté pan with the olive oil and on it arrange a layer of half the broccoli pieces, still wet from the washing. Scatter half the leeks, followed by the onion slices, anchovies and parsley on top and season with a generous amount of pepper and only a little bit of salt because remember the anchovies are quite salty. Repeat the layers with the remaining ingredients.

Cover the pan and cook over a low heat for 25–30 minutes. Add the wine, increase the heat and cook uncovered for a further 10 minutes. Allow nearly all the liquid to evaporate before serving.

Serves 4

4 tablespoons olive oil

1.5kg (3lb 5oz) broccoli, trimmed, broken into florets and washed

6 leeks, trimmed, cleaned and sliced lengthways

1 large onion, sliced

12 anchovy fillets (*I use the ones in oil, but if you have the salted ones in brine, soak and drain them first*)

30g (1¼oz) coarsely chopped parsley

salt and pepper

100ml (3½fl oz) dry white wine

Potato Pie

This is a very early recipe using potatoes, and comes from a nineteenth-century writer called Dr Kitchener in his *Book of the Cook's Oracle*. It uses that much-loved Georgian condiment, mushroom ketchup. You can buy this in bottles in delicatessens and I think it makes all the difference to the pie, but you can leave it out if you prefer.

Preheat the oven to 180°C/350°F/gas mark 4. Arrange the potatoes in layers in a pie dish. Between each layer of potatoes scatter some chopped onion and egg yolk and season with a little salt and pepper. (The egg yolks are optional in case you think cooking eggs is against the spirit of this book, if so, leave them out.) Put in about 2 tablespoons water and dab the butter over the top.

Roll out the puff pastry and cover the whole dish with it, sealing the edges and making a slit in the centre to let out the steam. Bake for about 1½ hours in the preheated oven. When the pie is ready, pour the mushroom ketchup through a funnel into the pie, as if you were putting the jelly into a pork pie.

Serves 4

1kg (2¼lb) potatoes, peeled and thinly sliced

1 small onion, finely chopped

4 hard-boiled egg yolks, coarsely chopped (optional)

salt and pepper

60g (2½oz) butter, cut into small pieces

1 packet of puff pastry

1 tablespoon mushroom ketchup (optional)

Mexican Corn Pudding

I find this is a very useful recipe as an accompaniment to cold meat, but for the purposes of this book it's a vegetarian recipe and it stands perfectly well on its own.

Preheat the oven to 160°c/325°f/gas mark 3. In a large mixing bowl, lightly combine all the ingredients except the polenta and the butter. Add the polenta and stir in with a large spoon until well mixed through. Grease a 1.5 litre (2½ pint) casserole with a little of the butter.

Let the remaining butter soften and add it to the mixture. Stir well, put the whole lot into the casserole and cook in the preheated oven for about 1 hour or until it is firm.

Serves 6

300g (10½oz) sweetcorn kernels (*if you're not keen on stripping sweetcorn cobs, you can use frozen or tinned corn*)

2 eggs, mixed together

300ml (10fl oz) milk

250g (9oz) tomatoes, skinned, deseeded and chopped

1 small onion, chopped

1 green and 1 red pepper, deseeded and cut into strips

75g (3oz) ripe olives (*with or without the stones removed, depending on how energetic you're feeling*)

salt and pepper

paprika

½ teaspoon chilli powder

175g (6oz) polenta

125g (4½oz) butter

Stuffed Tomatoes

For this you will need large, firm tomatoes. I don't really like those beef tomatoes because they never have very much taste but they are ideal for this kind of dish. In this recipe the tomatoes are stuffed with couscous, which keeps to the one-pot rule of this book and makes quite a substantial dish. You can always prepare extra couscous to serve on the side, if you like.

Preheat your oven to 190°C/375°F/gas mark 5. Slice a 'lid' from each of the tomatoes and then carefully scoop out the interior. Because I quite like tomato seeds, I tend to mix the pulp and the seeds with the couscous but you may want to discard them. Sprinkle the inside of each tomato with a little salt and set them upside down to drain.

Add boiling water to the couscous, according to the instructions on the packet. Then crumble your bread and mix it with the couscous, garlic, spring onions, anchovies, sultanas and parsley. Season this mixture and then stuff it into your tomatoes. Pop their lids back on, arrange the tomatoes in an oiled baking dish and cook in the oven for 20–25 minutes.

Serves 4

8 large, firm tomatoes

salt and black pepper

125g (4½oz) couscous

100g (3½oz) stale country bread

2 garlic cloves, crushed and worked into a paste with a little salt, or very finely chopped

bunch of spring onions, cut into small pieces

60g (2½oz) anchovy fillets in olive oil, mashed

30g (1¼oz) sultanas

2 tablespoons chopped parsley

Tomato Tart

If you grow tomatoes, there will come a time when you get a glut, and this is a particularly good way of using it up. If not, do your best to find fine, ripe tomatoes, not squishy but ripe. Be sure to smell them, even if they're in plastic - a tomato that's ripe has a wonderful earthy smell.

Preheat your oven to 230°C/450°F/gas mark 8. Put your baking sheet into the oven to heat up so that your pastry doesn't get a soggy bottom. Put your quartered tomatoes in a colander, season them and leave to drain. Roll the pastry out thinly and use it to line a 23cm (9 inch) fluted tart tin with a removable base. If you don't have one with a removable base, line the tart tin with greaseproof paper or baking parchment.

Sprinkle the pastry evenly with a third of the grated cheese. Mix the remaining cheese with the butter and cream into a paste, then beat in the eggs and season lightly. Spread your tomatoes evenly over the base of the pastry and spoon the egg and cheese mixture over the top. Put the tart on the hot baking sheet in the oven.

After the first 5 minutes, reduce the temperature to 200°C/400°F/gas mark 6 and then after another 5 minutes, turn it down to 180°C/350°F/gas mark 4 and continue to bake for another 30 minutes, until the filling is puffy and coloured and smells gorgeous and the pastry is crisp. If the pastry begins to burn before the tart is done, put some aluminium foil over it to protect it. Serve with a green salad.

Serves 4-6

750g (1lb 10 oz) ripe, firm tomatoes, skinned, seeded and quartered

salt and pepper

175g (6oz) pastry (*this should be rough puff but you can't buy that, so use shortcrust*)

100g (3½oz) Cheddar cheese, grated (*not too strong, or it will take away from the tomatoes*)

30g (1¼oz) softened butter

4 tablespoons double cream

2 eggs, lightly beaten

Cornish Onion and Apple Pie

This recipe comes from one of my great heroines, Dorothy Hartley, whose iconic book, *Food in England*, would almost certainly be my choice for a desert island book. I keep this by my bed and it is infinitely fascinating. I think some of her recipes are recorded for posterity rather than for eating, but this tasty dish is not one of them.

Preheat the oven to 190°C/375°F/gas mark 5. Roll your pastry out thinly and line an 18cm (7 inch) flan tin with it. Arrange a layer of apples on the bottom, then add a layer of onions and sprinkle with some of the sage and spice, and season. Build up with alternate layers until you've used up all your filling, then dot the top with butter or Cornish cream.

Cook in the oven for about 1 hour. If the top begins to darken too much, cover it with aluminium foil.

Serves 4

250g (9oz) shortcrust pastry

500g (18oz) cooking apples, peeled, cored and finely sliced

500g (18oz) onions, sliced into thin rings and then chopped

2 teaspoons finely chopped sage (*use dried sage if you haven't got any fresh*)

¼ teaspoon mixed spice

salt and pepper

3 tablespoons butter or Cornish clotted cream

Pumpkin Stew

At various stages in my life I've been exposed to pumpkins. Cooking as crew in the West Indies, where they use a lot of pumpkins, especially in the French islands, and when I was having a little diversion in Quercy, where they cook them with tomatoes. So this is really a combination of both, if you like.

Preheat the oven to 200°C/400°F/gas mark 6. Toss the pumpkin pieces in the flour, using it all up. In a heavy, ovenproof casserole, heat the oil, add the pumpkin pieces and sauté these over a medium heat for about 10 minutes. Then add the garlic and herbs, season and cook for a little longer. Add your tomatoes and cook for about another 5 minutes, until the tomatoes begin to soften.

Pour in the hot water and wine vinegar. Mix everything together well. Sprinkle the breadcrumbs over the top, dot with butter and cook for 20 minutes in the oven.

Serves 4

750g (1lb 10oz) pumpkin, peeled and cut into 2.5cm (1 inch) cubes

2 tablespoons flour

3 tablespoons olive oil

2 garlic cloves, crushed

1 tablespoon finely chopped parsley

good sprig each of marjoram and thyme, or ½ teaspoon if dried

1 bay leaf

salt and pepper

500g (18oz) tomatoes, sliced

300ml (10fl oz) hot water

1 tablespoon white wine vinegar

40g (1½oz) dried breadcrumbs

25g (1oz) butter

Ratatouille

I ate quite a lot of ratatouille when I was Lord Rector of Aberdeen University because it seemed to be the staple diet of students, especially towards the end of term when they were running out of money. And of course they would put anything into it that was cheap and they could get their hands on; no doubt it kept them regular. But this is the proper, Niçoise ratatouille. Don't peel your aubergines completely – leave some strips of skin to add colour and texture.

Heat your olive oil in a heavy pan and cook the onions, covered, for about 10 minutes or until they're soft and beginning to colour. Add the tomatoes and cook for a few more minutes, then add the courgettes, aubergines and peppers. Then add the garlic and bouquet garni and adjust the seasoning.

Cover and simmer over a low heat for 1 hour or until the vegetables have released their liquid and softened and blended. Take off the lid and cook for another 20–30 minutes to reduce the liquid. If you prefer, you can add your courgettes halfway through, which will mean they have a firmer texture.

Serves 6

1 dessertspoon olive oil

500g (18oz) onions, chopped

3 tomatoes, skinned, deseeded and chopped

500g (18oz) courgettes, sliced

500g (18oz) aubergines, partially peeled and sliced

3 red peppers, deseeded and cut into strips

1 garlic clove, crushed

1 bouquet garni

salt and pepper

Braised Bean Curd

I'm actually a great fan of bean curd, or tofu; I particularly like the smoked and fermented ones. In my case I like it with meat, but I find it makes a really good staple on its own. This is a simple braise but none the worse for that. As for an accompaniment, I leave that to you, but, for the purity of this book, it's actually quite nice with couscous.

Cut your bean curd into 2cm (¾ inch) pieces and leave on a double thickness of kitchen paper for 5 minutes to drain the excess moisture. Then sprinkle with a little salt and leave for another 10 minutes.

In a large, heavy frying pan, heat the oil and brown the bean curd pieces over a moderate heat. Add the soya sauce and all the other ingredients and bring to the boil. Then cover the mixture and simmer over a low heat for 10 minutes until a lot of the sauce has been absorbed. Try to make sure that all the bean curd is immersed; if not, you might have to move it around a bit to make sure it's cooked. Very simple!

Serves 4

250g (9oz) bean curd

salt

3 tablespoons vegetable oil

3 tablespoons soya sauce (*the Japanese variety is good for this*)

3 tablespoons water

1 teaspoon chilli powder

1 teaspoon crushed sesame seeds

1 garlic clove, crushed

3 spring onions, sliced

20 very thin slices of chilli

Mother Tante Pis Fondue

A fondue is, if you think about it, a one-pot meal, and this particular dish was always part of my youth. Fondues were great fun because every time you dropped your bread into the pot, you either had to buy a bottle of wine or kiss the man sitting next to you. In my case, the bottle of wine always seemed rather more attractive than the man beside me. This particular version of the fondue comes from Edouard de Poumon and the name of Mother Tante Pis, whoever she was, always appealed to me. You will need an earthenware or a metal dish, or, if you happen to have one, a fondue set.

Rub the inside of your fondue pot with the cut side of the garlic clove. Pour in the wine and season with the pepper and nutmeg. Add the cheese and bring to the boil over a medium heat. Cook for 8–10 minutes. The cheese will begin to melt and the wine to turn milky. The two tend to remain obstinately separate but don't worry because this is where the potato flour comes in.

Pour in the potato flour and wine mixture a little at a time, beating as you go. The mixture thickens and the wine blends with the cheese. Add the Kirsch and continue to stir. Boil for 1 minute, stirring all the time. Taste it and if the alcohol is too strong, cook for about 5 minutes longer; taste it again and if it's fine, set the pot on a spirit burner to keep it just bubbling.

Each guest should have about 20 pieces of dried bread, fairly thick but the size of a mouthful. You spear the bread on to a long-handled fork and dip it into the pot. Many romances have arisen out of the eating of fondue.

Serves 4

1 garlic clove, halved

300ml (10fl oz) very dry white wine

ground white pepper

good grating of nutmeg

400g (14oz) Gruyère cheese, cut into small pieces

½ teaspoon potato flour, mixed with 2 tablespoons white wine

3 tablespoons Kirsch

day-old bread, cubed

bottles of wine, for purchasing on the side, and several delectable members of the opposite sex

Savoury Bread Pudding with Asparagus

This is a delicious spring bread pudding, best cooked in May when British asparagus is in season; buying foreign asparagus is neither good for the planet nor does it taste good. The types of bread you use alter the texture of the dish, so try to use a cross-section varying from sourdough to focaccia to make it more interesting.

Place the bread in a shallow dish and pour on the milk and water solution. Leave to soak for 30 minutes.

Preheat the oven to 180°C/350°F/ gas mark 4. Trim the asparagus stalks, then cut them in half lengthways and into 5cm (2 inch) lengths. Wring out the bread. There should be 125ml (4fl oz) liquid left; if not, make it up to that amount. Beat the eggs and salt and pepper into the milk.

Butter a 3 litre (5 pint) ovenproof dish. Put one-third of the bread into the dish and layer half the asparagus pieces on top, scatter with half the herbs and one-third of each of the cheeses and the egg mixture. Continue with additional layers, finishing with bread, the remaining egg mixture, and finally cheese.

Dot with the butter and cook in the preheated oven for about 45 minutes until brown and crusty on top and an inserted knife comes out clean.

Serves 4

12–16 slices of mixed stale bread

600–700ml (1–1¼ pints) milk and water, mixed half and half

500g (18oz) asparagus

5 eggs

salt and pepper

8 tablespoons chopped herbs (*use a variety*)

4 tablespoons grated Pecorino cheese

125g (4½oz) Fontina cheese, thinly sliced

125g (4½oz) Gruyère cheese, thinly sliced

10g (½oz) butter, cut into small pieces

Risotto

A risotto is the most perfect one-pot meal. It does require a little more attention than some of the dishes in this book, but is excellent when you get home and discover you haven't got anything to eat and somebody's dropped in. It is terribly easy to make. You can conjure up risottos with absolutely anything that takes your fancy, so I'm just going to give you a basic risotto recipe.

In a sauté pan, heat the oil and cook the chopped onion and the mushrooms. Cover the pan and cook for about 12 minutes over a low heat. Scatter on the herbs. Add the rice to the pan and stir it so that it is well coated in the oil, at which point start to add the stock.

Add a little bit of stock and stir until the rice has absorbed it. Keep adding stock in this way until it has all been absorbed. When the rice is cooked, al dente but not too dry, remove the pan from the heat, add the butter cut into little pieces and the Parmesan cheese. Stir and serve at once.

Serves 4

2 tablespoons olive oil

1 onion, quite finely chopped

175g (6oz) mushrooms, chopped

2 tablespoons chopped mixed parsley, tarragon, chervil and chives, or any other herbs you happen to have

400g (14oz) risotto rice

1.5 litres (2½ pints) stock

50g (2oz) butter

60g (2½oz) Parmesan cheese, grated

A Pilaff of Bulgur Wheat

This Turkish dish is one that can be vegetarian. I'm just going to give you a fairly straightforward recipe but then you can use your imagination to bulk it out. It is a good, filling dish and one that responds well to extra ingredients. For instance, try adding sweetcorn, aubergines, spring onions, puntarelle mushrooms, green beans or baby broad beans.

Melt 30g (1¼oz) of the butter in a heavy saucepan and sauté the onion and leeks, stirring constantly, until the onion is golden brown. Add the tomato purée and the diced tomatoes and cook for about 5 minutes.

Pour on the stock, stir in the rest of the butter and season with salt and pepper. Bring to the boil, add the bulgur wheat, stir once, cover the pan and boil for 5 minutes. Then turn the heat down and continue to cook, covered, until the bulgur wheat has absorbed all the stock. This should take about 25–30 minutes.

Remove the pan from the heat, uncover it and place a napkin or sturdy kitchen paper over the saucepan and replace the lid. Leave this to stand in a warm place for about 40 minutes before serving.

Serves 6

75g (3oz) butter

1 large onion, grated or finely chopped

2 leeks, cleaned and cut into strips

1 tablespoon tomato purée

2–3 tomatoes, skinned, deseeded and diced

350ml (12fl oz) vegetable stock

salt and pepper

175g (6oz) long-grain bulgur wheat, washed and drained

PUDDINGS

Pershore Plums

Pershore in Worcestershire has always been renowned for its plums but today people don't really know what to do with plums, so I recommend this recipe to you. Using plums of different colours makes the dish more attractive, but it doesn't matter if you can't get a variety.

Preheat your oven to 160°C/325°F/gas mark 3. Halve the plums lengthways and remove the stones. Butter a large, shallow dish (you can use a baking tray lined with foil but an oven dish is better). Lay out the plum halves in close rows, cut sides upwards, red at one end and yellow at the other. Sprinkle the cinnamon and nutmeg on each half and then sprinkle thickly with two-thirds of the sugar.

Bake uncovered in the preheated oven for 35 minutes. Take the dish out and drop a walnut or an almond into each plum half. Sprinkle with the remaining sugar and return to the oven for a further 5 minutes.

Remove the dish from the oven. Leave it to cool and then refrigerate for at least 1 hour. Decorate with whipped cream and enjoy it.

Serves 4

750g (1lb 10oz) red plums
(*Victoria plums are good for this*)

750g (1lb 10oz) yellow plums
(*greengages or golden gages are good*)

10g (½oz) butter

½ teaspoon ground cinnamon

½ teaspoon freshly grated nutmeg

175g (6oz) caster sugar

100g (3½oz) shelled walnuts

60g (2½oz) blanched almonds

300ml (10fl oz) double cream, whipped just to hold a peak

Claret Jelly

My sister-in-law, Mara, gave me the recipe for this wonderfully fragrant and beautifully coloured jelly. I allow the wine to boil because you burn off the alcohol, but even then a lot of my friends who are also non-drinking don't feel comfortable around it. It is, I think, a typical late eighteenth-century recipe and you can use both port and claret together, if you want, although I tend to use just the claret.

One of the most embarrassing things I ever did was during a demonstration in quite hot weather. I had made one of these jellies in advance but, given the weather, had added extra gelatine so that it would stay set. When I went to turn it out, it took me four goes to get it out of the mould! You can have a lot of fun with choosing your moulds. Jelly moulds are easy to come by, so try to get an interesting one to make this pudding in.

Put all the ingredients into a saucepan with 150ml (5fl oz) water and stir until it comes to the boil. Continue to stir and cook for 2–3 minutes. Make sure that all the gelatine is dissolved, both the jelly cubes and the powdered or leaf gelatine. Pour the mixture into a chilled mould and leave in the refrigerator for at least 6 hours before unmoulding.

To unmould, submerge the outside of the mould in very hot water, almost boiling, and then turn out on to a plate.

Serves 4

850ml (1½ pints) reasonable but not expensive claret

1 packet of blackcurrant jelly

60g (2½oz) powdered or leaf gelatine, soaked in warm water

90g (3oz) caster sugar

½ teaspoon ground cinnamon

¼ teaspoon freshly grated nutmeg

juice of 1 lemon

Cheshire Cheese and Tablet Tart

To my mind, one of the most innovative and best cooks working today is Scotland's Sue Lawrence, and this recipe, which I have created from two of hers, uses Cheshire cheese in a sweet tart. In the original, called Chocolate and Grimbister Cheese Tart, Sue used cheese from Orkney which you can't really buy in the rest of the UK. I was planning a dinner I was to cook in Cheshire for the Cheshire cheese people, using cheese in every course, and remembering that Sue had made a cheesecake with tablet (a form of fudge) and cheese, as well as a chocolate tart, I rather combined the two and came up with this pudding. But let's make no bones about it, the whole concept is Sue's and she very kindly said that I could use it.

To make the pastry, put the flour, almonds, sugar and butter in the food processor and blend until it resembles breadcrumbs, then slowly add the beaten egg. Or, if you prefer, you can, as I do, make the whole thing by hand. Bring the dough together, wrap in clingfilm and chill for about 1 hour.

Roll out the pastry and use to line a 23cm (9 inch) tart tin. Prick the pastry all over with a fork and refrigerate for 2 hours or freeze for 30 minutes.

Preheat the oven to 200°C/400°F/gas mark 6. Line the pastry case with foil and, if you have them, with baking beans and bake blind for 15 minutes. Remove the foil and the beans and bake for 5 minutes more. Leave to cool for 10 minutes and then place on a baking sheet. Reduce the oven temperature to 180°C/350°F/gas mark 4.

Serves 6

200g (7oz) tablet (*or fudge if you can't get tablet; the better the quality of the tablet, the better the pudding will be*)

125g (4½oz) Cheshire or Wensleydale cheese, grated

1 large, egg

2 large egg yolks

100ml (3½fl oz) double cream

100ml (3½fl oz) milk

75g (3oz) caster sugar

For the pastry

150g (5½oz) plain flour, sifted

50g (2oz) ground almonds

25g (1oz) caster sugar (*Sue recommends that you use the golden non-bleached one*)

75g (3oz) butter, cut into cubes

1 large egg, beaten

Break the tablet into large chunks, put it in a food processor and grind it until it resembles breadcrumbs. Add the cheese, egg and yolks, cream, milk and sugar and continue to blend until it is well mixed. Pour into the pastry case. The case will be very full so be careful not to spill it.

Bake for about 30 minutes or until just set in the middle. There should still be a tiny wobble if shaken lightly. Leave for 30 minutes and serve barely warm.

Janet's Yogurt and Lemon Curd Pudding

This is a standby of a friend of mine and is quite delicious. It isn't actually cooked at all, so is well within the confines of one-pot cooking. It keeps for ages, so you can make it even a couple of days before your party.

Blend the yogurt, lemon curd and lemon juice together thoroughly and put it in the fridge to chill. I sprinkle the top with soft brown sugar, which goes slightly caramelised and I think makes it even more delicious.

Serves 4

400g (14oz) tub natural Greek yogurt

75g (3oz) lemon curd

juice of ½ lemon

soft brown sugar to serve (optional)

Orange Tart

This eighteenth-century recipe was supposed to be a favourite of Charlotte of Mecklenburg, wife of George III. It's an excellent pudding to have in your repertoire because you can get oranges all year round and therefore serve it at any time of the year.

Pre-heat your oven to 300°F/150°C/gas mark 2. Roll out the pastry and line a 24cm (10 inch) tart tin with it. Grate the peel and squeeze the juice from the oranges and lemon into a bowl. Beat the egg yolks well. Stir them into juice and peel together with 175g (6oz) of the sugar. Beat well and pour into the pastry-lined tin. Bake in the oven for about 45 minutes or until the mixture has set.

Beat the egg whites with the remaining sugar until they form soft peaks. Remove the tart from the oven, spread the meringue quickly on the top and return to the oven for 10 minutes until the meringue is crisp and lightly brown on the outside but soft on the inside. Serve at once.

Serves 4

250g (9oz) shortcrust pastry

4 oranges

1 lemon

6 eggs, separated

200g (7oz) caster sugar

Magic Chocolate Pudding

When I was small we were always told by Louise, our cook, that this was magic pudding because although you mix it all together, it magically separates out so that in the end you have a rich chocolate sauce at the bottom of the dish and a sponge cake at the top.

Preheat the oven to 180°c/350°f/gas mark 4. Grease a 1 litre (1¾ pint) ovenproof dish. In a bowl, cream the butter, sugar and egg yolks together until they are light and fluffy, then stir in the milk. Sift the flour and the cocoa powder together over the creamed mixture and beat it in until it is all evenly mixed. Whisk the egg whites until they are stiff, then fold them into the mixture and put the whole lot into your prepared dish.

Bake in the oven for 35–45 minutes until the top is set and spongy to the touch. Serve hot.

Serves 4

50g (2oz) butter

75g (3oz) caster sugar

2 eggs, separated

350ml (12fl oz) milk

40g (1½oz) self-raising flour

5 teaspoons cocoa powder

Rice Pudding

Rice pudding is a perfect one-pot dish, whether cooked on top of the stove or in the oven. This is a Portuguese recipe called 'sweet rice' or 'arroz dôce'.

Pour the milk into a pan and bring it to the boil. Add the rice and sugar and when the milk returns to the boil, add the lemon rind. Turn down the heat and cook the rice for as long as it takes to absorb the milk, usually about 20 minutes. Then remove from the heat.

Beat the egg yolks together and add them to the pan with a good pinch of salt. Stir well and return to a slow heat until the egg yolks are cooked. Transfer to a serving dish and sprinkle with cinnamon.

Serves 4

700ml (1¼ pints) milk

250g (9oz) pudding rice

250g (9oz) caster sugar

rind of 1 lemon

3 egg yolks

pinch of salt

ground cinnamon

Sussex Pond Pudding

This curious dish, obviously native to Sussex, needs a thin-skinned lemon that will burst inside the pudding during cooking, forming 'the pond' when you cut open the dish for serving. This was something that fascinated me as a child and I have loved it ever since.

Butter a large pudding basin with the softened butter. Roll out the suet pastry to 2cm (¾ inch) thick, make a circle for the lid and use the rest to line the pudding basin.

Cut the cold butter into 8 pieces and put 4 into the basin with half the sugar. Prick the lemon all over with a skewer so that the juice can escape. Stand the lemon vertically in the sugar and butter, then mould the rest of the sugar and butter around it. Cover with the pastry lid, dampening the edge and pressing down well to seal. Cover with aluminium foil and place a saucer that fits the top of the basin over the foil.

Place the basin in a large pan and pour water around it to a depth of 3cm (1¼ inches). Bring to the boil, put on a lid and keep just boiling for 3 hours, adding more water as needed.

Remove the saucer and the foil, invert the basin on to a large plate and serve with cream.

Serves 4

10g (½oz) softened butter

350g (12oz) suet pastry (see page 127)

125g (4½oz) unsalted butter, chilled

175g (6oz) demerara sugar

1 large, juicy, thin-skinned lemon

Apricot and Cardamom Flan

This is an unusual dish, the cardamom pods and bay leaves lending it a curiously subtle flavour. If you don't want to make the pâte sucré, then just use shortcrust pastry. You will bake your pastry blind in its tin, which means lining the tin with the pastry and then covering it either with baking beans or aluminium foil to stop the pastry rising and becoming uneven while it is cooking.

To make the pâte sucré, sift the flour and the salt into a bowl. Make a well in the centre and add the sugar, butter and egg yolks. Using your fingers, pinch and work the sugar, butter and eggs together until well blended. Gradually work in all the flour to bind the mixture together. Knead lightly until it is smooth. Wrap in clingfilm and leave in the refrigerator or a cool larder for a minimum of 30 minutes, or overnight if possible.

Put the apricots, cardamoms and bay leaves in a bowl. Cover with cold water and leave to soak overnight in a cool place, or in the refrigerator.

Preheat the oven to 190°C/375°F/gas mark 5. Roll out the pastry and line a 34×11cm (13×4 inch) loose-bottomed tranche tin (a rectangular flan tin). If you don't have one of these just use an ordinary flan tin but one with a detachable bottom. Chill this for 10–15 minutes and place on a baking sheet. Prick your pastry all over and then bake blind for about 20 minutes.

Serves 4

100g (3½oz) dried apricots

6 green cardamom pods, split

2 bay leaves

150ml (5fl oz) single cream

1 egg

1 egg yolk

25g (1oz) caster sugar

4 tablespoons apricot jam

For the pâte sucré

150g (5½oz) plain flour

pinch of salt

75g (3oz) caster sugar

75g (3oz) butter, at room temperature

2 egg yolks

Drain the apricots and throw away the bay leaves and the cardamom pods. Cut the apricots in half and dry them on kitchen paper. Whisk the cream, eggs and sugar together. Arrange the apricots, cut side down, on the pastry case and pour over the cream mixture.

Reduce the oven temperature to 180°C/350°F/gas mark 4 and bake for 35 minutes or until just set. Brown under the grill, then allow to cool. Mix the apricot jam with a little boiling water to dissolve it and brush over the flan to glaze.

Omelette Stephanie

We all know that the suicide pact of the Austrian Crown Prince Rudolph and his mistress Mary Vetsera, who died together at Mayerling, led indirectly to the outbreak of the First World War, the resulting changes in Europe and the deaths of thousands of its sons. There have been plays, films, novels and even a ballet on the theme. What is less well known is that Prince Rudolph had a wife, the Crown Princess Stephanie, whose legacy is a much better one. It is this delicious soufflé omelette.

Preheat the oven to 190°C/375°F/gas mark 5. Melt the butter in a fireproof dish and turn it to spread the butter evenly around the bottom. Beat the 3 egg yolks with 2 tablespoons of the icing sugar until the mixture is pale and forms ribbons. Beat in the double cream and the flour and fold the mixture into the egg whites.

Transfer the whole lot carefully into the hot buttered dish and cook it in the oven for just over 15 minutes, until it is well risen and lightly browned on the top. In the meantime, roll your raspberries in the remaining icing sugar.

Slide the omelette on to a warm plate, put the raspberries on one half and fold over the other half. Sprinkle with icing sugar and serve at once.

Serves 4

2 tablespoons butter

3 egg yolks

3 tablespoons icing sugar

3 tablespoons double cream

2 tablespoons plain flour

4 egg whites, stiffly beaten

1 large punnet of raspberries

Christmas Pudding Ice-cream Bombe

This is something different for Christmas and it's a pudding I made for the Winchester Choir boys in the first Christmas Special of *Two Fat Ladies*. I had to stand in front of the Aga in the Bishop of Winchester's kitchen and it was the hottest Aga I've ever come across. Everything was melting as I was doing it – including myself! But hopefully you won't have all the difficulties I had, nor, indeed, a perfectionist Welsh television director standing over you.

Fill the lower part of a double boiler with water, put the milk and half the sugar in the top. Bring it to just below boiling point. Beat the egg yolks and the remaining sugar in a bowl until pale and forming ribbons. Bring the milk to the boil and pour it in a thin stream on to the egg yolks and sugar, whisking steadily. Return this to the double boiler and stir the custard until it thickens to form a clear line when cooling on the back of the spoon. Plunge the base of the pan into cold water to stop it cooking further.

Transfer the custard to a jug, cover and chill. When the custard is cold, pour in the chilled cream. Stir the brandy into the custard and churn in an ice-cream mixer until it is the consistency of whipped cream, or transfer it to the freezer and give it a stir after 10 minutes. Crumble in the Christmas pudding and churn for a further 5 seconds, then freeze for 1–2 hours.

Serves 4

350ml (12fl oz) whole milk

100g (3½oz) soft brown sugar

3 egg yolks

175ml (6fl oz) whipping cream, chilled

1 tablespoon brandy

150g (5½oz) Christmas pudding

2 tablespoons brandy butter

1 tablespoon brandy, for serving

Fill the chilled bombe mould. Top with the brandy butter and close the mould. Allow this to freeze hard – overnight is best. To serve, turn it out on to a dish, pour the brandy over and set fire to it.

You might think that this slightly breaks the one-pot regulations but in fact the only cooking is done in your double boiler. Everything else involves freezing.

Orange Cream

This is an eighteenth-century recipe, referred to in Gervase Markham's *The English Housewife* (1615), an example of the white cream of the Middle Ages known as White Leche; 'leche' means 'sliced' and you cut the curd into slices. I find it a most unusual and delicious pudding. Curd is the set part of milk products either when they're cooked or when rennet has been added to them, and whey is the leftover liquid that remains once the curd has set.

Grate all the rind from both lemons and put it into a saucepan with 1.8 litres (3 pints) water. Add the sugar when the water becomes hot. Once the sugar has dissolved, allow to boil for 4 minutes. Remove the pan from the heat and set aside to cool slightly for 1 minute.

Beat the eggs into 600ml (1 pint) of the cream, then slowly stir in the hot syrup, always stirring in one direction. Allow the mixture to stand undisturbed in a cool place for 2 hours. Use a perforated slice to lift the curd into a colander and leave it to drain and set. Discard the whey.

When the curd is set, turn it on to a dish. Mix the orange flower water with the remaining cream and put it around the base of the curd. Decorate with crystallised orange slices and serve very cold.

Serves 4

- 2 lemons
- 90g (3oz) caster sugar
- 4 eggs
- 850ml (1½ pints) double cream
- 2 tablespoons orange flower water (*you can buy this in a delicatessen; or 1 tablespoon orange curaçao makes a good alternative*)
- crystallised orange slices, for decoration

Index

Page numbers in *italic* refer to the illustrations